inspired West Coast HOMES

Designed by Dworsky Architecture, page 31

Distinctive Homes Curated by Leading Architects, Designers, and Custom Builders for Coastal Living Lifestyles

Intermedia Publishing Services Inc
Dallas, TX 75252
972.898.8915
www.inspiredintermedia.com.com

Publisher: Brian G. Carabet
National Publisher: Marc Zurba
Managing Editor: Katrina Autem
Editor: Lindsey Wilson
Art Director: Brian Carabet
Production Coordinator: Vicki Martin

Copyright © 2024 by Intermedia Publishing Services Inc
All rights reserved.

No part of this book may be reproduced or transmitted in any form or by any means, electronic or mechanical, including photocopying, recording, or by any information storage or retrieval system, except brief excerpts for the purpose of review, without written permission of the publisher.

All images in this book have been reproduced with the knowledge and prior consent of the professionals concerned and no responsibility is accepted by the producer, publisher, or printer for any infringement of copyright or otherwise arising from the contents of this publication. Every effort has been made to ensure that credits accurately comply with the information supplied.

Printed in Malaysia

PUBLISHER'S DATA

INSPIRED WEST COAST HOMES

ISBN 13:   979-8-9877941-2-8

First Printing 2024

10 9 8 7 6 5 4 3 2

This publication is intended to showcase the work of extremely talented people. The publisher does not require, warrant, endorse, or verify any professional accreditations, educational backgrounds, or professional affiliations of the individuals or firms included herein. All copy and photography published herein has been reviewed and approved as free of any usage fees or rights and accurate by the individuals and/or firms included herein.

Intermedia Publishing Services is dedicated to the restoration and conservation of the environment. Our books are manufactured with strict adherence to an environmental management system in accordance with ISO 14001 standards, including the use of paper from mills certified to derive their products from well-managed forests. We are committed to continued investigation of alternative paper products and environmentally responsible manufacturing processes to ensure the preservation of our fragile planet.

Designed by First Lamp Architects, page 153

Designed by ORR Design Office, page 93

introduction

West Coast design is driven by sunshine, a moderate climate, and a freedom to create and experience nature as a part of the living space. Other areas of the country tend to rely much more on traditional design choices–such as the antebellum Greek Revival vibe of the south or the more traditional, colonial look of New England.

The Pacific Northwest integrates more of the natural elements in the environment blending softly textured surfaces that fit nicely into primarily transitional and Northwest modern themes while in nature. It incorporates elements such as stone, wood, natural fibers, and features colors found in nature like blues and greens. As the Pacific Northwest is known for grey rainy days, utilizing natural lighting is also very important–incorporating many windows and skylights to bring natural light to a home.

California is all about invention. Faced with the crumbling missions that the early settlers encountered during westward expansion of the 1800s, it inspired the creation of a new style of architecture referencing Spanish colonial history. In addition, later this inventive spirit birthed the Craftsman and midcentury styles. Importantly, the three design movements placed value on incorporating natural elements, offering a distinct take on design that emphasizes a connection to nature. They maximize the favorable climate for outdoor living, an abundance of natural materials and textures, inventive craftsmanship, and its relaxed and easy style.

West Coast design, while anchored firmly in its roots, has also led the current design trend of modern homes. The Pacific Northwest and parts of Northern California accent these modern designs with more natural elements, while coastal California features more open, neutral minimalist, yet expansive spaces to allow the views and/or ocean to become the centerpiece.

This book, *Inspired West Coast Homes,* features the impressive work of professionals from diverse backgrounds, who effortlessly meet all the challenges of architecture and design to express a sense of style that's as unique as the people who call on them to build their home. It lays the foundation for inspiration through stunning images that present an insider's look into this iconic region's homes while providing the inside story on exactly what goes into building these residences.

Within this extraordinary collection, you'll find resplendent condos with captivating views of downtown Vancouver, palatial California desert retreats, beachfront homes inspired by the Pacific Ocean, and bold juxtapositions of seemingly conflicting styles that somehow blend effortlessly thanks to the experts featured in these pages. With properties from British Columbia to Seattle, Oregon, Northern California, and Southern California, these architects, designers, and custom home builders passionately redefine what it means to turn a house into a home.

Enjoy our presentation!

Brian Carabet

Brian Carabet
Publisher & CEO

"Our design philosophy centers around creating residences that are harmonious with their external environment as well as rich in comfort and experience for those who live inside."
– Michael Dunsmuir, Step One Design

Designed by Step One Design, page 152

Designed by Elyssa Contardo Interior Design, page 39

Designed by Joseph Farrell Architecture, page 73

Designed by JF Carlson Architects, page 43

Designed by David Pool Architecture, page 143

Designed by Nordby Design, Architecture & Interiors, page 113

Designed by RLB Architecture, page 47

contents

SOUTHERN CALIFORNIA 13

(fer) studio 15
Amit Apel Design Inc. 19
Dean Larkin Design. 23
Dworsky Architecture 31
Elyssa Contardo Interior Design 39
JF Carlson Architects 43
RLB Architecture. 47
Shelia Todd Interiors 55

NORTHERN CALIFORNIA 59

Blaine Architects 61
DiVittorio Construction Inc.. 65
DiVittorio Designs LLC. 65
JTM Interiors 65
DNM Architecture. 69
Joseph Farrell Architecture 73
Mahya Salehi Studio 77
Marc Newman Architect 81
Mark Horton / Architecture. 85
ORR Design Office. 93
Saikley Architects 103

OREGON 111

Nordby Design, Architecture & Interiors 113
Sheri DeGeer Home 121
SORA Design 127

WASHINGTON 131

Click Architects 133
CLT Design Build 139
David Pool Architecture 143
Donnally Architects 147
First Lamp Architects 153
Island Architecture 161
Kaplan Homes 161
MacPherson Construction & Design 165

BRITISH COLUMBIA 175

Cara Interiors. 177
DCYT Architecture 181
Hynesite Designs. 185
Intermind Design Inc. 189
Isometrix Design Inc 199
Step One Design. 203
Vineyard Development 209

MEET THE DESIGNERS 212

Southern California. 212
Northern California 213
Oregon. 214
Washington. 215
British Columbia 216

Photograph by Roger Davies and Adrian Van Anz

Southern California Homes

Designing a home in California can give you the best pallette of options due to the majesty of the landscapes you have to work with. From the rugged coastlines, snow capped mountains, to the towering redwoods and beyond, nature provides inspiration for some of the most innovative homes on earth.

Over the years, the spaces have always drawn parallels between architecture and language. To fully comprehend a language, you must understand the rules, and once you've mastered the rules—or become fluent—you can let the creativity flow. In that sense, we see our homes as poetry, carefully crafted to suit the homeowners.

Each single-family home is a built interpretation of the homeowner's lifestyle, the site dynamics, the necessary solutions, and sustainable ideals. The most successful home, however, will be the one that was designed by a team who intently listened to the clients and engaged them in the process. We balance design work, construction, and renovation, and keep the homeowners involved at every step. It's a critical aspect of our success as a firm and what makes dream homes into a reality.

In order to arrive at the perfect home, we let go of any preconceived style or look that we want to achieve. Everything must suit the homeowner, so we are flexible with our aesthetic. You'll see everything from modern to traditional in our portfolio, with a wide array of architectural elements and details with a wide array of architectural elements and details.

Dean larkin
Dean Larkin Design
Los Angeles, CA
see page 212

Ridge Line Residence, Lake Malibu/Agoura Hills, CA

(fer) studio

RIDGE LINE RESIDENCE
Lake Malibu/Agoura Hills, CA

The story of the Ridge Line Residence is one of client resilience and transformation. Originally occupied by a 1980s dwelling, the property, along with all the clients' belongings, fell victim to the devastating wildfires of 2018. Approximately one year following the tragedy, the homeowners enlisted the services of (fer) studio to reimagine the property as a contemporary homesite that would not only optimize the site's inherent opportunities but also offer innovative solutions to its constraints.

Nestled on a hillside, the site presented a number of challenges while also offering a commanding, 270-degree mountainous sunset view. The house's primary configuration as a semi-two-story linear floorplan imaginatively flows along the hillside, tracing the contours of the site. Guests arrive by ascending the driveway and are greeted by an exterior arrival courtyard shaped by the distinctive angles of the house as it conforms to the hillside and the pre-existing, expansive retaining wall. On the opposite side of the house, a spacious patio serves as an elongated outdoor living and dining area, offering breathtaking views of the evening sunset. Fundamentally, the architectural design, envisaged as a unified architectural encounter between site and structure (form and environment), was tailored to help transform the homeowner's unique lifestyle, encompassing musical pursuits, culinary endeavors, and meditative practices.
Photographs by Joshua White
Designed by (fer) studio, Los Angeles, CA, page 212

AMIT APEL DESIGN INC.

Maliview Estate, Malibu, CA

MALIVIEW ESTATE
Malibu, CA

Our design philosophy is "connecting people to the art of living," which is evident in our work at this modern equestrian villa, Maliview Estate. The home is a completely unique art piece set in the Malibu mountains just a few minutes away from the Golden Coast of Southern California, so capturing the harmony of the natural environment was important to make sure the home fit its surroundings. We served as both the designer and builder for this project, and our attention to architectural form and design was of the highest priority.

Accents of lavender on a palette of muted tones help create visual interest as well as a uniquely calming living space. In this estate, our firm's artistic touches are found throughout the design, and because of its aesthetic, eye-catching vibes, it should come as no surprise that we've created art galleries in Los Angeles and Las Vegas. The entire home is made up of carefully sculpted lines and natural elements. We only take on projects that pique our interest and present a chance to explore our team's creativity with the clear goal of letting clients connect to the beauty and the art of living.

Photographs by Linda Kasian
Designed by Amit Apel Design Inc., Malibu, CA, page 212

Scan this QR code to view more custom homes designed by Amit Apel

DEAN LARKIN DESIGN

Latimer Sanctuary, Los Angeles, CA

LATIMER SANCTUARY
Los Angeles, CA

The homeowners for this Rustic Canyon project are empty nesters who were looking for a house that suits their active lifestyle, offers 6,000 square-feet of living space, and captures the natural relaxing grace of the surrounding environment. We wanted to pay homage to the rich history of the canyon, including the Ray Kappe project that exists just above this site. My background helped to prepare me for the detailed and historic accuracy I needed here. I was able to filter the design through the architectural lens of the likes of Ray Kappe, Marshal Lewis, and Thorton Abell. Latimer turned into the sculptural statement that we were looking for but still steers away from the clichés of simple geometrical uniformity of modern architecture.

Latimer Sanctuary blurs the lines between what is organic and what is architectural and reveals a multi-layered complexity that appears equally effortless and elegant. Natural materials inside the house consist of walnut cabinetry and aged-oak floors and ceilings, which deliver warmth to the rooms. The design balances the warmth with a series of poured-concrete walls that seem to float in the localized "lake" arranged to give the homeowners privacy and separate public and personal spaces without jarring boundary walls. The lake element in the house joins the water outside to enter the house under the main stairs and further blurs the boundaries between inside and outside. The site included an existing sycamore tree, and we used that to anchor not only the lap pool but also the couple's primary bathroom and master suite, allowing them to swim their morning laps starting and ending through the large sliding wall of glass. Perpendicular to the lap pool is the great room with its corresponding covered loggia. The powder room offers a unique view of the pool and the eye-catching water curtain, a privacy screen of falling water that lets guests experience the home's architecture at an intimate scale. The house was placed toward the rear of the site, which meant we were able to create the upper bedrooms in such a way that allows them to exit onto their own terrace. Even guests in the home will feel the relief of having a private area to relax.

Staying true to my other residential designs, Latimer Sanctuary captures and utilizes the unique climate, attitude, and lifestyle of Southern California that makes the home feel completely natural in its environment.
Photographs by Roger Davies and Adrian Van Anz
Designed by Dean Larkin Design, Los Angeles, CA, page 212

Scan this QR code to view a video tour of this home with Dean Larkin

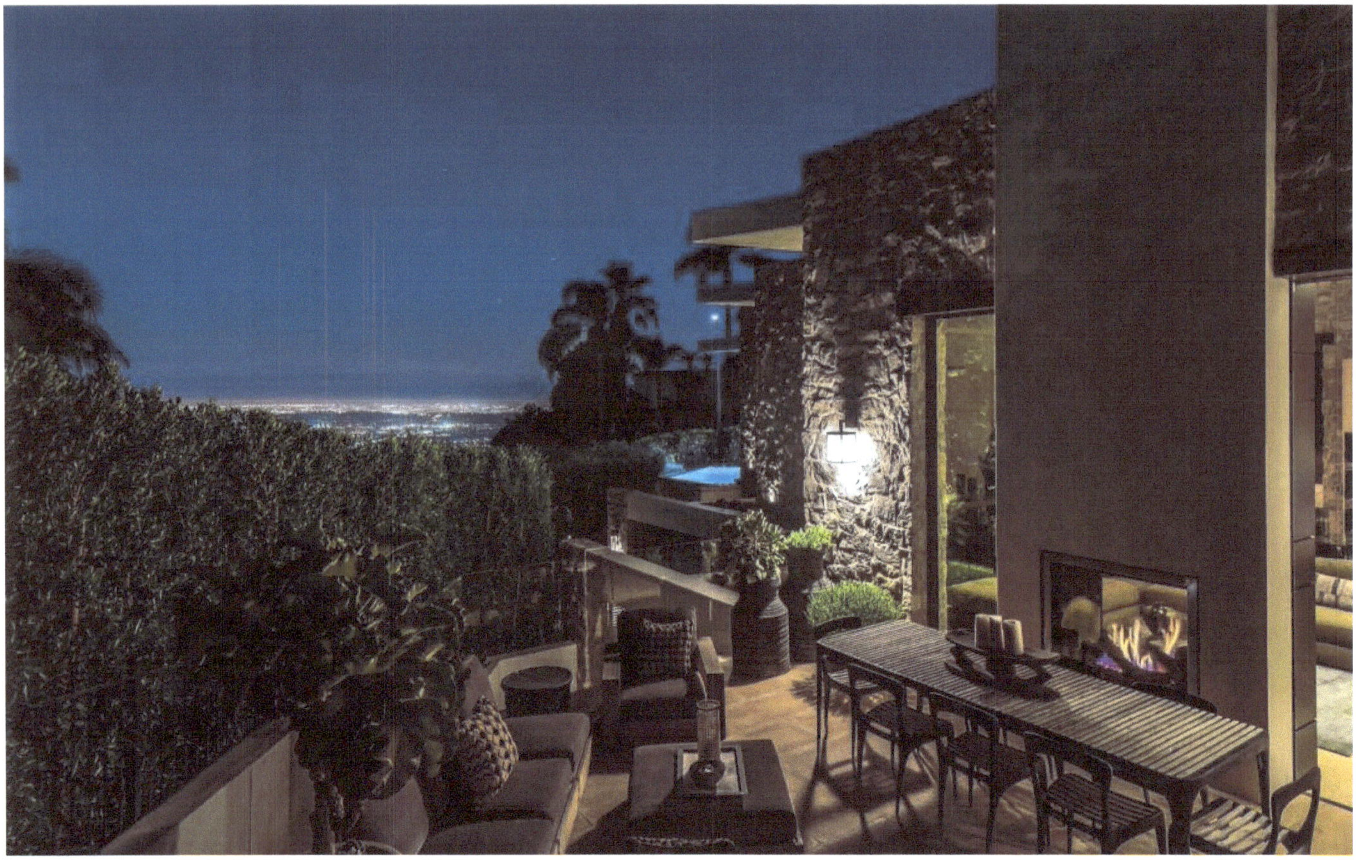

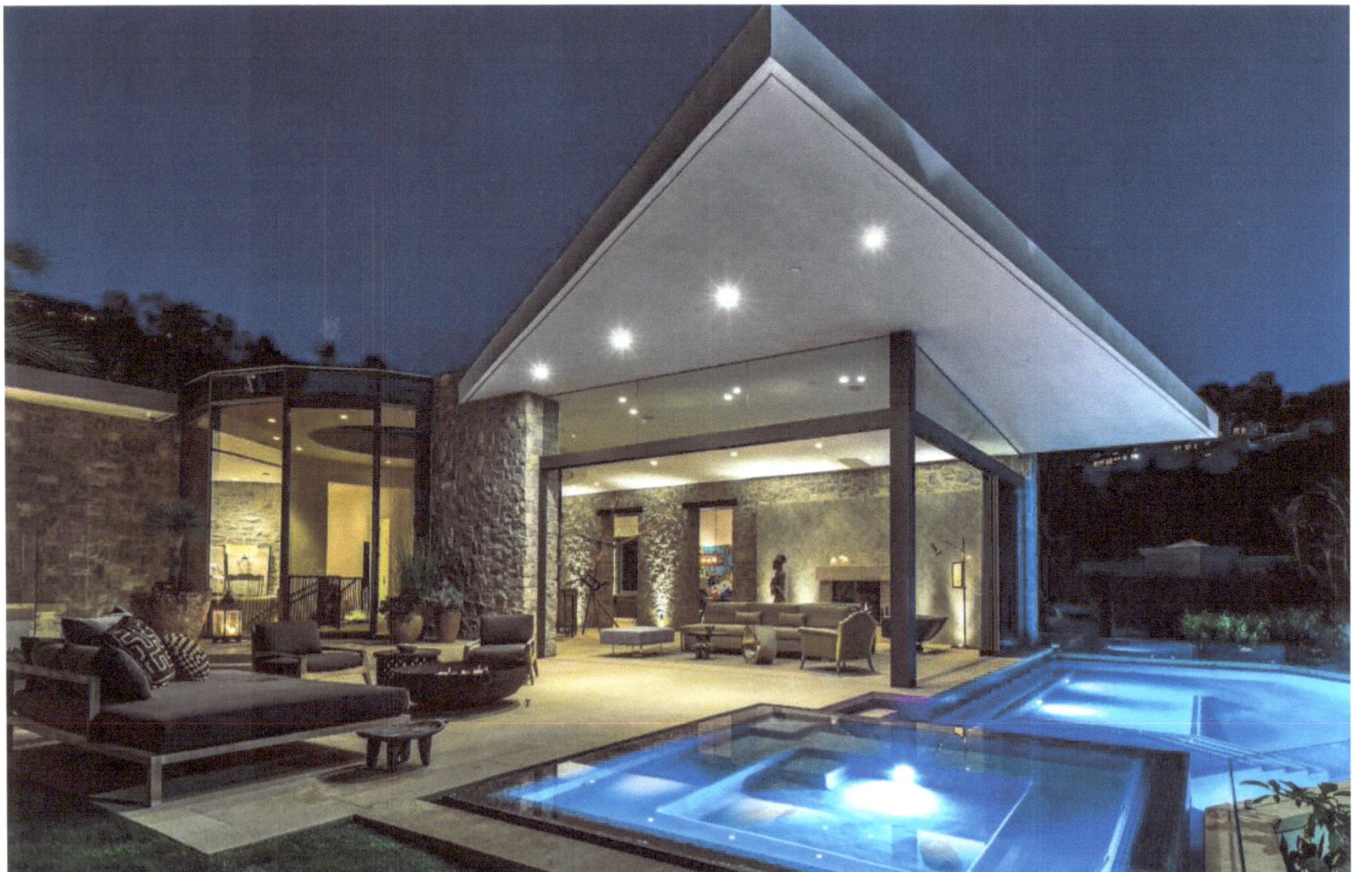

SWALLOW RESIDENCE
Los Angeles, CA

Located in the prestigious Bird Streets of the Hollywood Hills, near Sunset Strip in West Hollywood, our design for the Swallow Residence contains gestural, rusticated stone walls that serve as an important element both structurally and aesthetically. They rise beautifully from the site and break with the axis of the adjacent streets to run parallel to the view corridor on this interior corner lot. The walls form the parti for special ordering of the interior spaces. Public, communal rooms are wrapped around and through these walls, but the walls also amplify and focus the homeowners and their guests on the nearby city view.

In addition, the walls also serve to heighten the house's privacy from the surrounding neighbors on what was previously a very exposed corner property. Like most clients, these homeowners wanted some seclusion and solitude from the street and busy surroundings. Combined with angled roof lines that both whimsically tip and point to the view beyond, the walls also provide a crucial link between indoor and outdoor spaces, which is an ideal feature for entertaining friends and family and hosting large parties. Finally, the front and back yards meld together into one courtyard formed by the L-shaped house, maximizing space and view.

Photographs by Adrian Van Anz
Designed by Dean Larkin Design, Los Angeles, CA, page 212

DWORSKY ARCHITECTURE

Venice Beach Residence, Venice, CA

VENICE BEACH RESIDENCE
Venice, CA

Set on a small but prominent urban corner lot, this 3,700-square-foot residence creates a spacious living environment and a timeless architectural addition to the eclectic beach homes of Venice, California. The open, loft-like interior encompasses the entry, dining, kitchen, and lounge areas and connects to a small private yard through large sliding-glass doors. Each zone within the open areas of the home has been articulated by differing floor levels, finish materials, ceiling and lighting configurations, as well as window scale and orientation. We designed a rooftop deck with panoramic views that provides extended outdoor entertainment opportunities.

The double-height volume is the spatial focus of the home, encompassing the entry and dining areas and allowing natural light to extend deeper into the center of the house. The second-level walkway, home office, family room, and media room overlook this double-height volume, from which access is provided to three bedroom suites.

We wanted to create privacy on this prominent corner lot, which we've maintained by surrounding solid fences, carefully placed landscaping, and a raised-concrete planter at the entry. The exterior is articulated with a base of cedar siding supporting an upper mass of smooth integrally colored plaster. The second-floor windows lie primarily within a horizontal band, which is further articulated by corrugated metal panels encircling the perimeter.

Photographs by Natalia Knezevic

Designed by Dworsky Architecture, Los Angeles, CA, page 212

WESTWOOD RESIDENCE
Westwood, CA

The Westwood Residence sits on a typical mid-block site in a neighborhood filled with Tudor and Spanish-style homes. Built for a couple with two boys, the house provides an open living area and a broad spatial connection to its small, private rear yard on a sloping, restrictive lot. The architectural vocabulary of the home is both modern and timeless and is articulated by a palette of materials that provide a warm and intimate environment for its residents and guests. A mantra of "modern and cozy" was a constant theme through the design process.

Our design solution includes the creation of a three-level home on a site that slopes gently up from front to rear. The main level of the house is the second level, housing dining, living, and kitchen functions in a continuously open space that is level with the rear yard. Each area on this level is articulated with varying ceiling and lighting configurations, creating several varying zones within an otherwise open floorplan. Expansive wood-framed glass sliding door panels connect these spaces to the rear yard, which is defined by tall hedges and conceptualized as a "green" room. The top level of the house contains bedrooms and home offices, while the lower level contains the enclosed garage and a multipurpose playroom for children. A double-height living room is the heart of the home and visually connects the second and third levels. A dramatically curving wall leads from the entry through the main living area, reflecting how one moves through the home, and continues up through to the top level, dynamically connecting all the main spaces of the structure. Naturally colored oak and soft neutral tones dominate as a material theme throughout the home, from oak flooring, cabinets, and slats to light-colored quartzite counters and limestone wall cladding.

Photographs by Natalia Knezevic
Designed by Dworsky Architecture, Los Angeles, CA, page 212

Inspired West Coast Homes

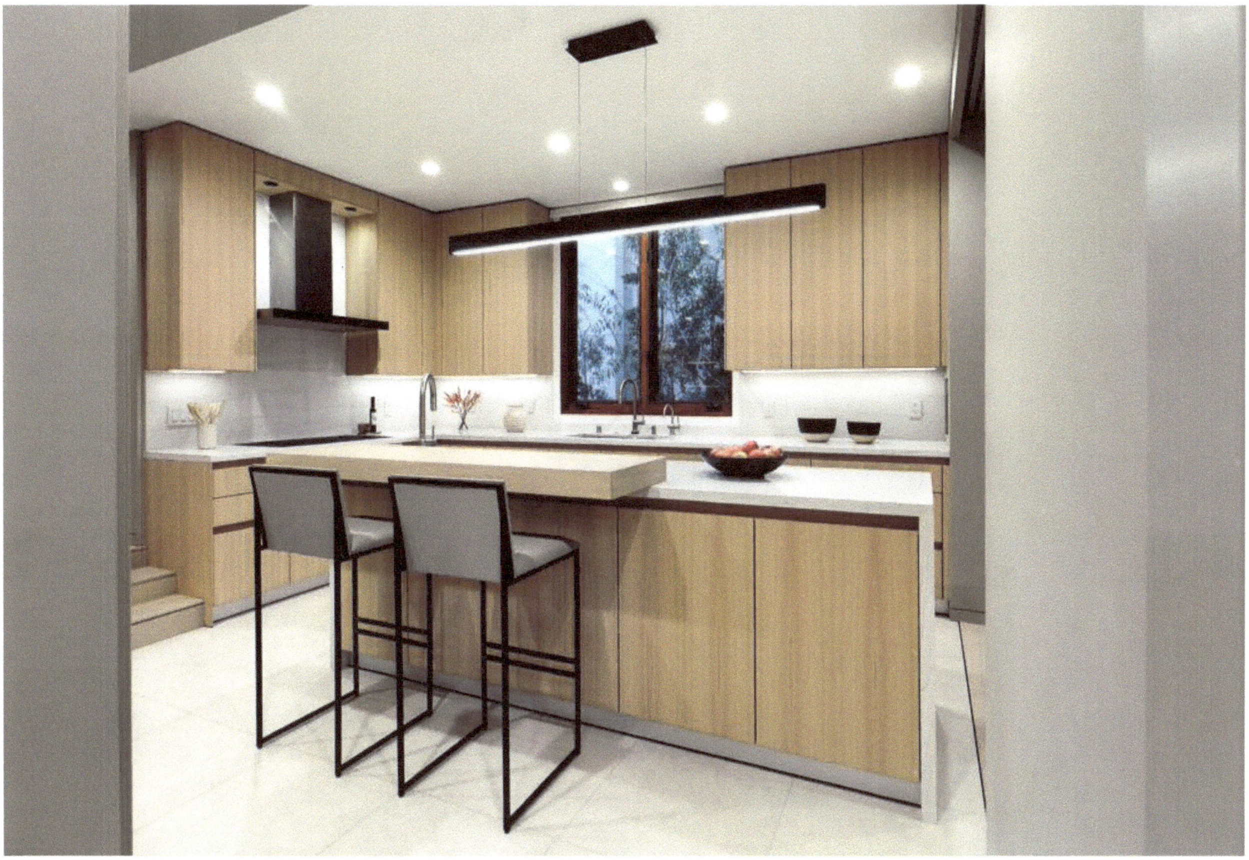

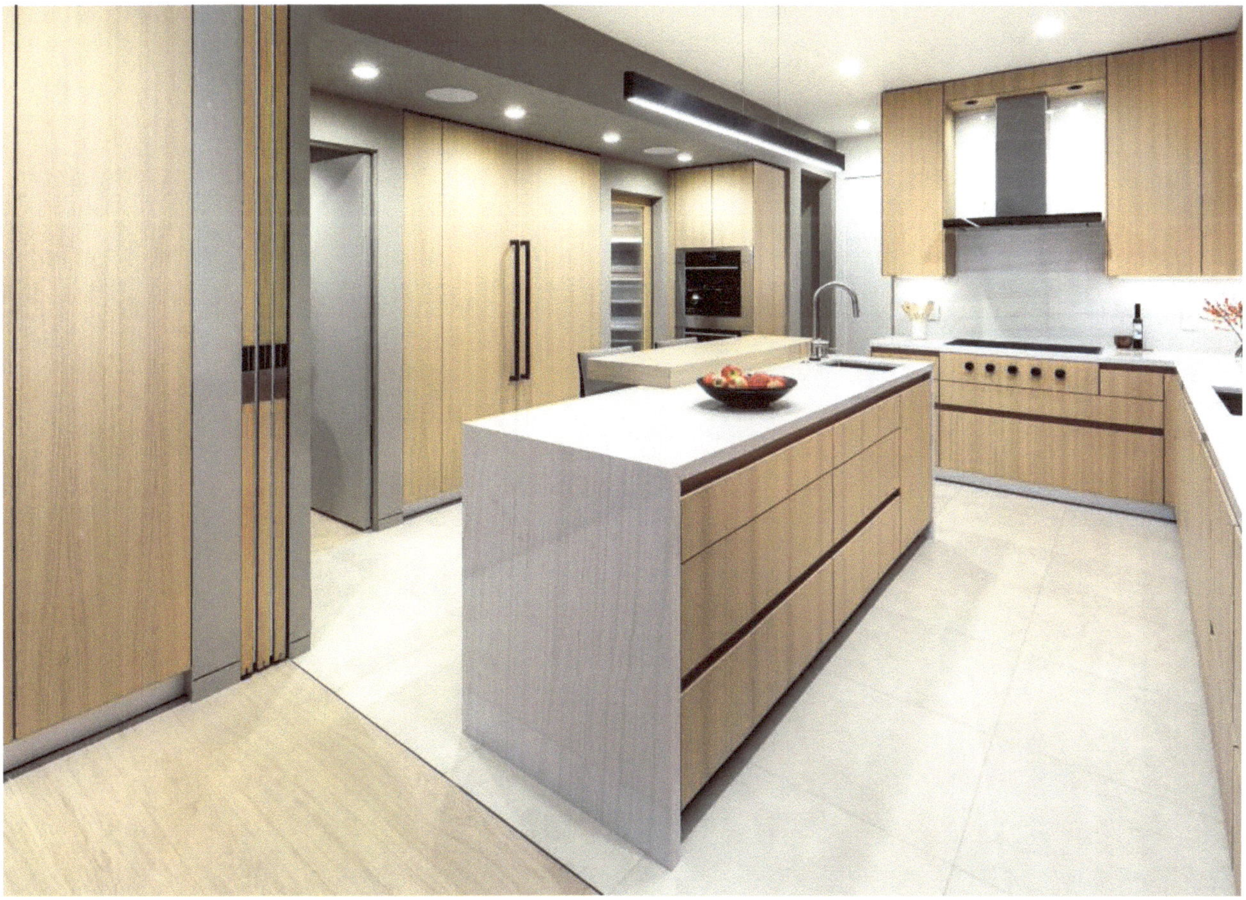

ELYSSA CONTARDO INTERIOR DESIGN

Domus Atticus Estate. Palm Desert, CA

DOMUS ATTICUS ESTATE
Palm Desert, CA

This desert hideaway ensures complete privacy and was a fully transformative remodel, from the entry gates to the interior layout and even the landscaping. The owner and developer, a Greek shipping tycoon, was intensely involved in the planning and gave valuable design input on everything from the flawless kitchen finishes to the updated landscaping. The outdoor makeover includes a new pool and entertaining pavilion, a private lake with boat launch, lighted tennis court, equestrian riding arena, and adding two large barbecue areas and loggias. At more than 10,000 square feet and sat on upwards of eight acres, the home has plenty of room to accommodate family, friends, and guests. Classic European style runs throughout the home, with lustrous wood floors and retracting glass walls allowing the nearby San Jacinto and Santa Rosa mountain views to shine. The neutral palette encourages the contemporary lighting, a lot of which is channel-set into the ceiling, to subtly add a modern edge. Though each room possesses its own impressive charm, the glass-enclosed wine room, bar and screening theater, and elegant library are all delightful surprises to discover when wandering the home. Two primary retreats even offer their own kitchenettes, palatial bathrooms, and direct patio access.

Photographs courtesy of Elyssa Contardo Interior Design

**Designed by Elyssa Contardo Interior Design,
Palm Desert, CA, page 212**

Scan this QR code to view more amazing homes designed by Elyssa Contardo

Inspired West Coast Homes

JF CARLSON ARCHITECTS

Newport Isle Waterfront, Newport Beach, CA

44   Inspired West Coast Homes

NEWPORT ISLE WATERFRONT
Newport Beach, CA

We created an entirely new home within the existing walls of this 1960s waterfront project. Working closely with the homeowners, we completed an extensive makeover to design an all-new interior and an exterior with modernized street and waterfront elevations for a revamped façade. The newly transformed house shows off a modern, open environment while capturing the picturesque features of its coastal location. Because the owners were happy with the basic structure of the house, we kept its best elements and expanded from there. In the end, we only added 200 square feet to the footprint. All the interior spaces were redesigned to provide a seamless, open great room that leads to the new waterfront deck. Electrical, mechanical, and plumbing was completely replaced, along with a new elevator and dramatic stairs to the second level. All, new interior walls and a new standing-seam metal roof were added. The second floor includes three new bedrooms, all with ensuite bathrooms. The primary suite features his-and-her closets and separate bathrooms. A full gym completes the second floor, with an open balcony shared by the master suite that features sightlines to the isle waterway. A new entry structure was also added to provide a private, secure, and open outdoor foyer to the main entry.

Because we specialize in designs that meet the clients' needs and wants down to the smallest detail, we are in the business of creating dream homes. I have no set style in mind and work to bring the homeowners' choices and desires to life.

Photographs by Jason Crane
Below photograph by James Carlson
**Designed by JF Carlson Architects,
Newport Beach, CA, page 212**

RLB ARCHITECTURE

A French Inspired Home., Pacific Palisades, CA

Inspired West Coast Homes

A FRENCH-INSPIRED HOME
Pacific Palisades, CA

Accessible design inspired much of this home's layout, from a pair of bedroom suites on the lowest floor to adequate wheelchair clearance in hallways, bathrooms, and shared living spaces. Both a staircase and an elevator connect all three levels, the top of which houses a trio of ensuite bedrooms with high, sloping ceilings to luxuriously house visiting family members. The rear of the house encourages indoor-outdoor living—the kitchen and family room have French pocket doors, for example—but it was imperative that we devise a privacy solution for the primary bedroom's terrace, which faces the property's front. Our solution was to enclose it with stone-faced walls capped with limestone to match the home's carved friezes and other stone architectural details. The primary bathroom is outfitted with electric glass windows that turn opaque via the flip of a switch. On the ground floor, the rooms open up toward each other, with the living room and library offering a cozy retreat thanks to their fireplace, built-in bookshelves, and wood paneling. In addition to the two suites, one fully wheelchair-accessible, the basement level also contains a media room, laundry facilities, and an outdoor stairway to the rear.

Photographs by Anthony Peres Photography

Designed by RLB Architecture, Pacific Palisades, CA, page 212

A MODERN EUROPEAN FARMHOUSE
Malibu, CA

The guest house here was constructed first so the owner could live on-site during construction of the main house. This meant we could accompany them to showrooms and stores to help with the selection of materials, later incorporating those choices into the drawings. With a design inspired by a Virginia hunting lodge, the home highlights European hardscaping across the 1.5-acre site, which slopes challengingly toward the rear yet needed to still provide clear fire department access. The main house is set back 200 feet, so visitors are gifted with a stroll through the lush garden as they approach the front entrance, which looks straight through to the back of the property. Inside, rare 17th-century oak imported from several European chateaus was used for the floors, while ceiling heights rise from 12-foot high walls. The gourmet kitchen was outfitted with a wood-burning fireplace oven, furniture-quality cabinets, zinc countertops, and a marble-topped island with a skylight directly above. A large, three-sided bay window was designed to accommodate a booth from the iconic and now-closed Chasen's, with an additional adjacent seating area nearby. In addition to a mechanical room, a wine cellar was constructed in the home's basement to accommodate the owner's vast wine collection.

Photographs by Anthony Peres Photography
Designed by RLB Architecture, Pacific Palisades, CA, page 212

SHELIA TODD INTERIORS

Lafayette Retreat, Lafayette, CA

LAFAYETTE RETREAT
Lafayette, CA

Our approach to design with this project was to create a sense of longevity by incorporating natural materials, antiques, and exquisite lighting for a personal touch. You can see all of those elements woven throughout the rooms, along with organic, calming tones and warm, welcoming materials. It gives the spaces an elegant but comfortable aesthetic. I try not to be swayed by trends but by using materials that reflect their home environment, and the use of the homeowners' original contemporary art and antiques is at the heart of each project.

The results of this approach are always unique and authentic, which my client so appreciates, and it offers a sense of timelessness to the design. I want to create an aesthetic that never gets old, never goes out of style. We worked closely and collaboratively with the homeowners to understand their needs and desires so that we could deliver a solution that excels in both form and function. I like to empower my clients to think mindfully about their home, often in a whole new perspective, and understand it as a foundation for happy and successful lives.

Photographs by Can Ahtam, @canahtam

**Designed by Shelia Todd Interiors,
Pacific Palisades, CA, page 212**

Photographs by Blake Marvin & Lisa Petrole

Northern California Homes

Designing homes for the individualists who live here is inspiring. There is a spirit of innovation and a risk-tolerant mindset that allows architects and designers to push the envelope. With a strong diversity of people and ideas, a rich Gold Rush history, and an agricultural bounty, Northern California is unlike any other place in the world.

Northern California has a casual yet refined architectural style that defines the region. It shies away from formality and Old-World European aesthetics as much as it does the ultra-modern white-box look of Hollywood. You'll find a simpler, more sophisticated style that favors indoor-outdoor living. As you take in the engaging homes on the following pages, keep this in mind, and notice the large walls of opening-glass doors and deep overhangs that offer sun protection, gardens and landscaped grounds that are responsive to the region, and the use of finished materials that flow from inside to the outside. These elements all play off of the the area's natural features. With those elements also comes influences from midcentury modern style, Bay Area shingle style, Central Valley's comfortable ranch-style homes, casual "modern agrarian barn" styles, and the Sierra Mountain styles.

Dramatic topography, the effects of climate change, an increase in wildfires, and state energy codes can present an array of challenges. These issues prompt us to think outside the box and helps raise the bar for problem solving. A broad range of climate zones can sometimes be difficult, but also allow us to embrace indoor-outdoor lifestyles in regions that include the coast and inland adjacent mountains, the expansive flat agricultural Central Valley, the low elevation Sierra Foothills, and the high Sierra's forested mountains. The diverse geography provides unlimited opportunities to design homes and outdoor landscape environments that uniquely respond to their specific locations.

Gary Orr
ORR Design Office
East Bay and Sacramento, CA
See page 213

BLAINE ARCHITECTS

Midcentury Goes Modern, Sunnyvale, CA

Scan this QR code to view a video about Blaine Architects

MIDCENTURY GOES MODERN
Sunnyvale, CA

How does one create something unique and different that still responds to a neighborhood's design intent? The homeowners' goal was an iconic Eichler home, and once a program and general layout for the 500-square-foot addition to the front was established, various roof shapes were explored as a way of differentiating the building. Instead of sloping up toward the center of the structure, the addition slopes dynamically up and away. It can be a challenge to add natural light into the center of the home with these smaller lots in Silicon Valley, because many homeowners' instinct is to overbuild their lot. As a contrast, many original Eicher homes embraced an open-air atrium entry, with glass walls on all four sides. Though the owner had purchased a non-atrium model, the front build-out allowed the original design to shift and accommodate a traditional open-air courtyard. The concept of this home is sleek, minimal, and clean, and every materiality decision embraces this ideal. Instead of the traditional mahogany, white oak is used. Large-format white terrazzo complements the warmth of the wood, while whitewashed cork flooring pays homage to the 1960s. Dimensional tile from Rombini adds depth and texture under the kitchen island and in the primary bathroom.
Photographs by Mariko Reed

Designed by Blaine Architects, San Jose, CA, page 213

DIVITTORIO DESIGNS LLC
JTM INTERIORS
DIVITTORIO CONSTRUCTION INC.

Ultimate Forever Family Home, Los Aktos, CA

ULTIMATE FOREVER FAMILY HOME
Los Altos, CA

When we renovated this Bay Area home, we evaluated our clients' needs and reimagined the entire property in its fullest potential. Our focus was to fully customize it to the homeowners who decided to make it their forever home. We wanted this house to feel like they designed it from the ground up while still adhering closely to the original footprint. We reconfigured the entire home into a space that was beautiful, practical, energy efficient, and could evolve with the family for years to come. Additional square footage in the kitchen allowed for improved functionality, as the space accommodates more than one cook. We chose nature-based design materials and finishes that were inspired by the family's interests in the outdoors. This allowed for increased natural light and a blurring of the lines between the indors and out.

While the kitchen is elegant, we kept the sunken living room family-friendly with plenty of space to read and play games. With flexibility to expand, the dining room can host large dinner parties, as the bi-folding door connects the outdoor living space to the indoors, further enhancing the nature-based design elements seen throughout the home.

Interior design by Janet Marena, JTM Interiors
Construction: Roy DiVittorio, Divittorio Construction, Inc.
Photographs by Agnieszka Jakubowicz Photography

Architectural design by DiVittorio Designs LLC, San Jose, CA, page 213

Deer Park, San Rafael, CA

DNM ARCHITECTURE

DEER PARK
San Rafael, CA

Located north of San Francisco, the Deer Park residence was designed and built for a sloped, V-shaped lot on a site was essentially divided in half by a natural depression in the land that served as a drainage system. The environment presented challenges for my team but also gave us an opportunity to build something completely singular with stunning views. Our approach for this home combines practicality and environmental sensitivity to make as little impact on the site as possible. The main dwelling is placed along the slope on the northeast side of the lot to minimize the grading and maximize the views of Mount Tamalpais to the southeast. On the southwest section of the property and the opposite side of the natural depression, a separate two-car garage and ADU sits and preserves the natural flow of water through the site. We organized the layout to provide a sense of procession, where visitors enter the property at one corner and eventually arrive at the opposite, discovering the modern interior spaces and grandiose views. There is a strong axis from the front door to the terrace. The home's driveway begins near the garage and runs almost flat along the edge of the property, parallel with the road, connecting the two buildings. We designed the house with energy efficiency and scenic views in mind. The implied hallway provides the central access point for all areas of the home and serves as the main artery of the layout. The upper level is a primary living space and where most of the day-to-day tasks take place.
Photographs by Jamie Leasure
Designed by DNM Architecture, Sausalito, CA, page 213

JOSEPH FARRELL ARCHITECTURE

St. Helena Residence, St. Helena, CA

ST. HELENA RESIDENCE
St. Helena, CA

St. Helena, California, is a picturesque setting, so when we designed this custom single-family home, we wanted to capture the full scope of the surrounding Napa Valley vineyards. To do this, we prioritized the importance of giving each space a dramatic view of the beautiful outdoor landscape. With the rear yard facing south, we also embraced the site's ideal solar orientation. The transitional architecture of the home embraces traditional forms with straightforward proportions, elements of symmetry, and structure. As you approach the home, the exterior immediately captures attention with its harmonious blend of rich cypress siding, local natural stone, and elegant metal roofing.

The heart of the home lies in its open-concept living spaces. The spacious great room is adorned with plush furnishings and a cozy fireplace, and serves as the perfect gathering spot for the family to unwind and share time together. We masterfully achieved a serene haven where the family can dine al fresco, enjoy leisurely afternoons, and revel in the surrounding beauty through the covered and screened loggia and the integration of interior and exterior spaces. Privacy and tranquility are preserved with a thoughtfully designed primary bedroom suite, offering a personal sanctuary for the young family of four to retreat and rejuvenate.

Interior design by Lyndsay Gerber Interiors
Built by Trainor Builders
Photographs by Nicole Franzen
Designed by Joseph Farrell Architecture, St. Helena, CA, page 213

MAHYA SALEHI STUDIO

Carolina Street Residence, Walnut Creek, CA

CAROLINA STREET RESIDENCE
San Francisco, CA

As you approach the entrance, a delicate balance between simplicity and purpose unfolds; we see a demise of well-defined entryways in the city as developments look to utilize every inch as interior space. We wanted to explore a porch design that is not grand in scale but has real personality. Here, it is quite minimal and practical while presenting a defining sensibility. As far as finishes, we started with a bright and neutral palette but incorporated vibrant graphic tiles in various areas to infuse the urban sanctuary with the personality of the homeowner.

Like many homes in San Francisco, the project abuts the neighbor at a blind wall. We turned the challenge of a windowless wall into a major design opportunity by stacking the three-story staircase in the core of the home and flooding the space with natural light through the two oversized skylights above. The light penetrates through the open risers and 40-foot vertical cable railings, creating beautiful and dynamic shadow patterns on the blind wall throughout the day.

We turned to warm, organic materials to define the entertaining spaces and then layered in an unexpected, moody moment with the all-black powder room. The portrait painting "Lesende" by Gerrard Richter is reflected in the antiqued mirror. In the dining area, the crisp, minimal interior lends itself to a bespoke art piece by San Francisco's very own Aaron De La Cruz. As the evening sun sets, the room becomes an oasis of inspiration and dialogue, merging art, design, and culinary memories.

Photographs by Suzanna Scott
Designed by Mahya Salehi Studio, Walnut Creek, CA , page 213

MARC NEWMAN ARCHITECT

Contemporary Residence & Pool House, Oakland, CA

CONTEMPORARY RESIDENCE & POOL HOUSE
Oakland, CA

We transformed an existing 1940s ranch-style home with a midcentury addition into a new, contemporary residence. With sustainable practices in place, we approached the project with net-zero energy goals. The entire house was taken down to the studs and redesigned with a new primary suite addition. The midcentury addition was beautiful, and we worked to preserve it as we designed and built around it. Reconfiguring the open floorplan with a new entry, kitchen, living, and family room so that they interact seamlessly was a primary focus on this project. A minimalist approach, clean details, and natural materials are vital to the overall design of this midcentury gem, which carried through in the creation of the new pool house and refurbishment of pool and patio.

The natural materials we chose, both inside and out, complement the lot's wooded setting and reveal my love of incorporating nature into a home. We chose passive house strategies to bring this home to the forefront of modern energy design. Photovoltaic panels, efficient HVAC systems, and high-performance building envelopes were utilized for energy reduction and overall thermal comfort. Sustainable, recycled, and renewable materials were installed to reduce our environmental impact with the project.

Photographs by Kurt Manley
Designed by Marc Newman Architect, Oakland, CA, page 213

MARK HORTON / ARCHITECTURE

Rotated Modern, Atherton, CA

ROTATED MODERN
Atherton, CA

On a relatively modest and oddly shaped parcel skewed to the street, a single-family home moderates between organizing axes by shifting the building grid between levels. At the interior of the house, the finishes are pared down to a neutral palette to allow the architectural elements to shine. European oak, white walls, exposed concrete, and no trim all reinforce the architectural aspect of the space. Profuse light from oversized windows and the second-floor atrium window fills the space to further accentuate the sculptural creation. The central interior helical staircase, set at the rotation point of the orthogonal structure of the house, allows this shift to work seamlessly. The three-story staircase atrium acts as the central element through which all the circulation feeds, allowing the 'spin" off this point to feel comfortable and effortless. The exterior of the house is clad in contrasting materials to reinforce the geometric shift. The ground floor is wrapped in a heavy, rough, white Texas limestone, while the hovering, rotated floor above, including the roof, is a homogenous element of a strongly contrasting, lighter-weight, black matte-finished, standing seam metal cladding. The large, exposed roof area of the main floor is covered in a green geometric pattern.
Photographs by Mariko Reed

**Designed by Mark Horton / Architecture,
San Francisco, CA, page 214**

HILLSIDE MINIMALIST
Los Gatos, CA

A new home in yet another planned development filled with homes aspiring to be sited in pre-modern Italy or Spain, this house is a breath of fresh California air. Spacious rooms seamlessly connect to outdoor terraces, complemented by expansive glass windows and doors which erase the line between indoors and out, as the landscape, the views, and the climate all would prefer. Sizeable raw concrete walls create a unity between the interior and exterior while also providing a tactile contrast with the sleek interior finishes. Skylights, as well as glass floor surfaces opening to the lower level, further this transparency between in and out in the vertical condition. The neutral interior finishes allow the spaces to read even more strongly as architecture, and the very large expanses of glass pour light into the interior in various ways. Depending on the time of day, the light alters the feeling and texture of the finishes and, as a result, the sense of space within the house. The entry side of the house presents a closed solid façade, while the rear of the house opens up and expands the living space out into the Silicon Valley below.
Photographs by Bruce Damonte Photography

Designed by Mark Horton / Architecture,
San Francisco, CA, page 214

HILLTOP HIGH-RISE
San Francisco, CA

A 270-degree view of the San Francisco Bay is difficult to beat, even with well-designed architecture. Vantages from this apartment high on Russian Hill take in everything from the Bay Bridge, Alcatraz, and Angel Island to the Golden Gate Bridge, the Marin Headlands, and Twin Peaks. The architecture complements the vistas. Bronze detailing, eucalyptus woodwork, and walnut floors all contribute to a subtle and pleasant palette that doesn't compete with the natural beauty beyond. Custom light fixtures, an organic-shaped wood-clad structural column, and a new fireplace all add to the composition. What's not apparent are the construction details required to bury the top and bottom window mullions, the soffitted mechanical diffusers, and the recessed trim throughout—all details that contribute to the clean, minimal finishes which remove the barrier between inside and outside and extend the living space into the environment beyond. A final nod to the view is the 33-foot-long wallpaper on the south wall of the apartment, showing the vantage in that direction as seen by the famous photographer Eadweard Muybridge, of stop-action horse photos fame. As the one panorama in the apartment that you can't actually see, this vista, circa 1878, completes the 360-degree view.
Photographs by Bruce Damonte Photography

**Designed by Mark Horton / Architecture,
San Francisco, CA, page 214**

ORR DESIGN OFFICE

Modern Residence For Art Collectors, St Helena, CA.

MODERN RESIDENCE FOR ART COLLECTORS
St. Helena, CA

"We are from Chicago and of course love architecture and design. We knew that we wanted a classic, modern style, California inside-outside house that was sophisticated and timeless. We entertain a lot and have friends over and also need places to display key pieces of our art collection."

Located in a quiet, mature neighborhood, our dreamhouse clients sought out a larger, flat lot with several existing mature trees that could allow the home to sprawl into the site and landscape. The result was an innovative layout on the axis of the compass—**north, south, east, and west**—that resulted in dramatic moonrises and sunsets that pass through the spaces differently each day and each season. We intentionally conceptualized the house and site layout to showcase specific pieces from the clients' art collection as a fundamental part of the building and landscape design. Each of the L-shaped house's ground-floor rooms access a rear "outdoor room" patio area that includes a spa-water feature, sunshade canopy, and linear fire pits for evening warming. Interior floors of pea-gravel terrazzo flow outside and use the same aggregates for the patio's exposed concrete paving. A front yard reflecting pool and frosted glass fence strategically hide interior views from the street.

Photographs by Blake Marvin & Lisa Petrole
Designed by ORR Design Office, East Bay & Sacramento, CA, page 214

CONTEMPORARY RANCH HOUSE
Danville, CA

"We have just two big dreams: We'd like to be able to see the majesty of Mount Diablo sunrises from our bed and want all the rooms to have lots of glass that will connect the interior to the outside. And our dogs are Labradors, so they want a swimming pool."

Located in a leafy, walkable neighborhood of pre-war-era California ranch homes, our clients decided to stay in place and support their long-term community relationships by removing their outdated 1940s home and redeveloping the site to preserve several mature oaks, a sycamore, and large redwood trees. The result is a wonderful, new, contemporary-style ranch home with a relaxed beauty that hides a design and technology fusion. The two-story home, over a street-level below-grade garage, steps up the sloping site and allows for connected interior-exterior spaces on every side of the home, including the second-floor owner's suite level that is partly set into the slope. A private central courtyard with pool, cabana, and covered fireplace patio seamlessly connects to the main house with bluestone pavers that are radiantly warmed by tubing with solar-heated water. Building materials and methods of construction were green-sourced, recycled, and environmentally healthy, earning the project the highest LEED Platinum certification.

Photographs by Lisa Petrole
Designed by ORR Design Office, East Bay & Sacramento, CA, page 214

THE ORBITAL
Sacramento, CA

"We love modern architecture but do not want to live in a big glass box. We prefer a signature design style of curves and softer-shaped spaces and open glass that brings a lot of light inside. Our extended family of 40 to 50 gathers for dinner once a month, and we need to accommodate everybody in a cozy way."

This creative project is a live-in sculptural experience. There are so many uniquely designed innovations that it is impossible to summarize everything unless an entire book was written about it—which was done. Features include sweeping curved walls that "flow" through the house into the site, a swimming pool, and patios; an intimate forest of trees that extends the front yard nearly to the house's core; and a 12-by-20-foot curved sliding wall that separates the living room and highly finished garage to become a huge temporary living room extension. A sweeping "sky bridge" in the backyard slopes around and above the pool, creating a second-floor ramped access way and dramatic spatial enclosure in the backyard. The design was blessed by a feng shui master that came from Hong Kong, who directed certain specific features to be developed so that health and prosperity would come to the family and their friends.

Photographs by Don Button
Designed by ORR Design Office, East Bay & Sacramento, CA, page 214

MODERN ITALIAN FARMHOUSE IN A VINEYARD
Sierra Wine Country, CA

"We want a barefoot house! We envision living in a vineyard, in a farmhouse—not an ancient, broken-down house or one of those suburban faux Mediterranean villas, but a modern European farmhouse that's fresh. We want it to feel new and old at the same time."

We loved designing this project because everything about it is about simple living. Less about building than creating a sense of place that would inspire informal gatherings with friends, fresh food, and a lifestyle that is connected to an agricultural landscape. Designed to appear as if different occupants had enlarged the original house over time, the wings of the house each respond to the adjacent landscape with vineyard-view patios, intimate courtyards, and commanding roof decks. The building materials of the house seamlessly flow into the exterior — colored concrete flooring, smooth stucco-plastered walls and fireplace, crafted concrete countertops, window frames color-matched to the oak tree leaves, terracotta-colored columns, chimney covers made from industrial vitrified clay sewer pipes, and metal roofing that matches the color of grape leaves. Technology abounds—floors are heated by radiant tubing imbedded in the concrete, air vents are hidden, natural cross-flow ventilation means air conditioning is rarely used, and music from the piano fills the home acoustically.

Photographs by Jay Graham
Designed by ORR Design Office, East Bay & Sacramento, CA, page 214

101

SAIKLEY ARCHITECTS

Hilltop Contemporary, Richmond, CA

HILLTOP CONTEMPORARY
Richmond, CA

When we designed a ground-up home atop the Richmond Hills, we worked closely with the owner-builder to create the 2,300-square-foot home. Despite the beautiful site with its panoramic 270-degree views, the sloping lot had been left undeveloped over the years due to its modest size and challenging approval issues. We handled the negotiations for county approvals and maximized the site's potential for the three-bedroom, two-and-a-half-bathroom family home. The first-time owner-builder, Tsering Denma of Shambhala Landscapes, is a landscape builder by trade, and we coordinated closely with him on this spec home. We came up with creative solutions to fulfill the complex zoning requirements. We also provided building design details, which Denma then carried through in many unique interior design and furniture details throughout the house. The landscape design by Denma graciously complements and enhances the building and its relationship to the site.

Photographs by Chi Chin Photography
Designed by Saikley Architects, Alameda, CA, page 214

 *Scan this QR code to view more custom homes designed by Saikley Architects*

MODERN MEDITERRANEAN
Mountain View, CA

Optimizing space was an important aspect of our design approach for the Modern Mediterranean home project. It allowed us to balance improved function and experience for the family with the city planning department's challenging criteria. In collaboration with contractor Mara Construction, the home's transformation entailed a gut remodel and second-floor addition, using a combination of contemporary architectural details and a Mediterranean aesthetic. It was a dramatic overhaul that completely changed the layout of the house. We spent a great deal of time with the family to get to know them and create the design together. Our results brought together form and function, with living spaces that flow and connect from inside to outside. The layout includes a sunny front-yard seating area off the kitchen where the family visits with neighbors, and a secluded rear patio and garden off the great room. The primary bedroom suite features a Japanese bath and a private roof terrace with built-in seating, which is screened from view by a trellis, plantings, drapery, and lanterns.
Photographs by Kurt Manley
Designed by Saikley Architects, Alameda, CA, page 214

BLUEBERRY HOUSE
Berkeley, CA

Set on any idyllic site in the lower Berkeley Hills next to Codornices Creek, this home has seen a lot of change—and ideas for change—over the years. With an understated front façade to the street, the house becomes tall toward the large backyard as the ground drops down toward the creek at the rear of the lot. Our clients bought the property for its tranquil forested setting and its walking proximity to the heart of Berkeley's civic and commercial areas. Primary concerns were accessibility for older family members and friends, accommodation of spaces for religious ceremonies and social gatherings, and a large addition with a flexible floorplan. The integration between house and site was always at the heart of the design. During construction, it became clear to our clients that a different property would better fit their needs, and so they sold this property when the house addition was partially built. We then worked with designer Tim Larkin of STG Engineering and the new developer-builder, Dan McDunn, on design revisions and permitting. McDunn largely kept our large, flexible floorplan and the landscape layout as we had developed, but he made some key changes to fit a broader market. McDunn designed the interior and exterior finish details, landscaping, and building systems, and finished building the project.

Photographs by Open Homes Photography
Designed by Saikley Architects, Alameda, CA, page 214

Photographs by Rummedia and David DeMille

Oregon Homes

Creating luxury homes in the Pacific Northwest gives us the advantage of having some of the country's most beautiful landscapes to use as backdrops. Natural beauty isn't something we, or any architect and or designer, can replicate, so we aim to simply incorporate it into our designs whenever possible. Bodies of blue-grey water, green rolling hills, massive evergreen trees, picturesque mountains—the Pacific Northwest, and in particular Oregon, has it all. Though large windows and far-reaching sightlines abound in our projects, it's impossible to forget the land's beauty.

Because of this, it makes sense to choose colors and materials that accentuate the environment and don't compete with it. You'll see plenty of organic elements such as wood, glass, and metal throughout our designs, and warm, calming colors that underscore the land and its features. Outdoor living spaces make sense with such picture-perfect surroundings, so many of our homes feature large porches, patios, and pools to maximize the use of the home's exterior and create a natural flow with indoor-outdoor living. Overhangs and covered areas often appear in our work too, allowing for gatherings and get-togethers during showers and storms.

Of course, Oregon's environmental elements can also present design and building challenges, which we're both experienced at and equipped to handle. Every successful project navigates through several complex phases, and environmental factors often play a big role in these. At Nordby Design, we take great pride in our ability to guide clients through the entire project, from concept through completion, with our knowledge and professionalism to deliver gorgeous, functional spaces that our clients love. Within the following pages, you'll see some of those projects, along with the work of other firms that design and build within the natural beauty of Oregon.

Jon & Julie Nordby
Nordby Design, Architecture & Interiors
Lake Oswego, OR
see page 214

NORDBY DESIGN ARCHITECTURE & INTERIORS

Sweetbrier Road, West Linn, OR

SWEETBRIER ROAD
West Linn, OR

Nestled in the heart of Clackamas County, this project was a high-end luxury home with a lot of space that feels cozy and warm. The layout is approximately 9,500-plus square feet on a beautiful five-acre parcel of land. We designed the house to take advantage of the tree-lined property facing south and a picturesque dry creek bed, maximizing the beautiful scenic setting. The home has two large bedroom suites on the main level, one at each end. As you walk into the entry, your eyes immediately go straight through the great room to the trees—a sight line that helps bring the outdoors in. Nature is an element in this home that appears in every room in some way, giving a sense of peace and tranquility to the spaces.

The sun-filled daylight basement has two bedrooms on one end and another suite at the opposite end. The family room, exercise room, wine room, and dry sauna is adjacent. Under the large four-car garage is a memorable entertainment space that includes a state-of-the-art movie room, arcade, and pool areas and an adjacent small lounge. All that area leads out to the covered patio with a full barbecue kitchen. The homeowners couldn't ask for a better space in which to relax, hang out, and enjoy family and friends.

Photographs by Rummedia and David DeMille

Designed by Nordby Design, Lake Oswego, OR, page 214

 *Scan this QR code to view more homes by Nordby Design, Architecture & Interiors*

CLARKHILL ROAD
Portland, OR

With sweeping southern views of the valley, this luxury custom home sits on more than 11 acres, at an impressive 12,000 square feet. We wanted to maximize the stunning surroundings and used the idea of incorporating the views as the main component when designing. There are two levels in this layout, plus a small daylight basement. On the main level you'll find communal spaces such as the great room, kitchen, dining room, office, kids' study, kids' playroom, an over-sized laundry and craft room, plus an expansive four-car garage with space to spare.

The upper-level houses all four of the bedroom suites, with the primary suite attached to a large deck that covers the main-level outdoor dining area. Over the large garage is a spacious teenager recreation area and useful home storage. The daylight basement has a guest suite and spa area, a movie theater room with a pool table, plus a wine and whisky bar with a cozy sitting area. A covered area is just outside and doubles as the main-level covered-outdoor living space above. At the heart of the home's floorplan, we used two axes: one from the entry through the great room and covered patio to the green views of the valley, and the second, perpendicular to the primary axis that is the pathway to other areas of the home. The backyard boasts a tranquil in-ground swimming pool and surrounding entertaining areas for plenty of year-round outdoor fun.

Photographs by David DeMille

Designed by Nordby Design, Lake Oswego, OR, page 214

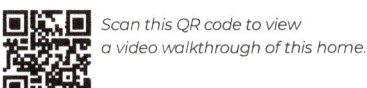
Scan this QR code to view a video walkthrough of this home.

BURTON STREET
Portland, OR

The original 1960s Burton Street home was outdated, so our clients chose to completely demolish it and design a new luxury single-level home. We focused the new design around the existing, now-updated in-ground pool. Many of our new homes are centered around axes, focal points, and key elements that define the design. This home was no exception and was created with an axis from the main entry that extends through to the center of the pool. The house wraps around the pool with covered living areas that offer entertainment spaces for every season. We chose striking white stucco and brick facades, plus a black metal roof, to give the exterior modern, clean lines to match its modern European aesthetic. The color contrast is eye-catching, stunning, and refined without being dramatic.

The 8,000-square-foot, single-level design sprawls out on the two-acre property in a sparsely populated, picturesque neighborhood of Northwest Portland. It's the ideal house for residents who value privacy, entertaining guests, and having space for their hobbies. It has four full bedroom suites, an open great room with plenty of space to gather, a kitchen and dining area, and a roomy man cave and entertaining room that provides a calm, relaxing environment. There is also a connected office and greenhouse, a workout room, and a large three-car garage.

Photographs by David DeMille

Designed by Nordby Design, Lake Oswego, OR, page 214

SHERÍ DEGEER HOME

Hilltop Respite, Happy Valley, OR

HILLTOP RESPITE
Happy Valley, OR

Situated at the top of the hill of Happy Valley, this traditional Oregon residence has breathtaking panoramic views of Portland. My team and I were given carte blanche to design a masterful home filled with all the charm of Italy. The home was built by a Street of Dreams Builder and was already 10 years old when we began our work. In the primary suite, the clients wanted a cheerful room with tones of yellow. As a certified color expert, I leveraged my knowledge of color psychology to create a palette that not only brightens and warms the Northwest's winter days but also fosters a sense of comfort. Motorized blackout silk draperies frame the unmatched views of Mount St. Helens and the city lights, while radiant heated floors on Picasso travertine adds warmth underfoot for chilly mornings. Appealing to the family's heritage, I designed the room with a Mediterranean flair. From the meticulously hand-painted ceiling replicating Italian tiles to the Jerusalem stone in the steam shower, the primary suite delivers on character. Each room throughout the house was a work of art, completely custom in every detail. When the couple asked me to create extraordinary guest spaces, I came up with some fantasy concepts which include the Lodge, Bahama, and Spa rooms. These rooms have proven to be timeless, as guests of all ages love staying there. I always use a very personal approach, even in guest spaces.

The lower-level family room area, which was remodeled for the empty nesters' growing family, is complete with rich, durable, hickory hardwood floors and stylish interior masonry that adds character to the intimate wine cellar. A space was created for games, where you can challenge loved ones to chess while enjoying the twinkling city lights below. Additionally, a home gym was added, which takes advantage of the Portland vistas. To arrive at the right style, I got to know the homeowners and examined their daily lives. I asked myself what would make them say, "I love living here." I almost always focus on shapes and textures, intentionally mixing masculine with feminine elements. In every case, I focus on lighting, color, and scale. Getting color right is critical by itself. I don't like rooms that are too perfect; it is important that they feel comfortable, approachable, and interesting. I have a keen eye for detail and love collaborating with local craftsmen to transform homes and lives. I create timeless designs that increase a home's value.

Photographs by Crosby Dove Photography
Designed by Sherí DeGeer Home, Beaverton, OR, page 214

SORA DESIGN

Gallery House, Ridgefield, WA

GALLERY HOUSE
Ridgefield, WA

The idea of the Gallery House, a new construction, began with the clients' primary objective, which was to take the advantage of the breathtaking view to the northeast of Mount Adams and Mount St. Helens. The concept that we brought to the table was the creation of corridors that extend the line of sight through the house in both directions. These generous corridors allow light and air to flow freely throughout the house and allowed us to divide the home into several programmatic volumes: semi-public space, the gym and office; private space, the primary suite; public space, kitchen, living room, and dining room; and the garage. These become evident from the exterior as layered volumes from all sides of the house.

Inside, while the active views toward the mountains are dramatic, the long passive views through the house are soothing to the eye. The generous corridors give the sense of simple luxury. In addition, the views through windows and spaces create a layering effect on the inside of the house. Outside, the layering of volumes and material adds depth and interest. The simple rooflines are dramatic and there are unique perspectives from all sides of the house. A challenging part of the design was that the couple came from different backgrounds and had competing thoughts on what feels like a home. It was a discovery process for both, and the project was unified with mutual interest in the use of natural materials, stucco, multiple building volumes with vaulted ceilings, and the wish to invite natural light and views into the spaces.

Photographs by SORA design
Designed by SORA design, Portland, OR, page 214

Washington Homes

Architecture in Washington State is quite diverse. In general, the technology industry has varied the population, bringing in a wide range of cultures and styles, and therefore created a unique opportunity for a large variety of architectural styles to flourish.

The region's natural beauty, focus on sustainability, and environmental sensitivity heavily influence our architectural vernaculars. The use of indigenous materials such as wood and stone create an appealing, organic palette. We even extend this philosophy to the furniture we hand select for homes. Additionally, the weather suggests covered patios that extend the season and windows to let more sunlight in during the darker days.

Specializing in waterfront construction, we are regularly challenged by the topography leading to the lakes. Ensuring the homes flow downhill and managing all the possible effects, is always a priority. Creative solutions for dealing with access to the home and the water, plus the area's topography, are always something we have to consider, as would any architect or builder in this environment. The solutions become creatively integrated into the homes we design.

Our projects are primarily focused in the Eastern Puget Sound area, and our uniqueness is found in the ability to manage and perform everything from the dream's inception to full construction, no matter how challenging the dynamics may be. On the following pages, you'll see the reward of all our hard work, along with other firms'—Washington homes filled with happy clients who share their home with family and friends.

Roger MacPherson
MacPherson Construction & Design
Sammamish, WA
see page 215

Broadview Residence, Seattle, WA

CLICK ARCHITECTS

BROADVIEW RESIDENCE
Seattle, WA

We believe that every project provides a conduit for the exploration of human experience as it relates to the built environment and the emotional response to a specific space, and the Broadview Residence is no exception. Located on a busy street in north Seattle, the home was designed to create a private and relaxing oasis for the homeowner. Our primary goal was to create a home that complemented the scale and fabric of the existing neighborhood while providing a private, south-facing courtyard that takes full advantage of natural light and extends the interior living space.

The home is designed with strategically placed public spaces, including a formal entry courtyard arranged near the street, acting as a buffer for the remainder of the home. Utilizing the natural topography allowed us the opportunity to explore spatial volumes by varying ceiling and floor heights. A subdued interior material palette aids in creating the peaceful environment. Stained cedar walls cleverly conceal the home's storage areas. A rooftop deck is positioned at the highest point on the site, maximizing western views of Puget Sound and the Olympic Mountains.

Photographs by Will Austin Photography
Designed by Click Architects, Seattle, WA, page 215

CLT DESIGN / BUILD

Wiser Lake House, Wiser Lake, WA

WISER LAKE HOUSE
Wiser Lake, WA

Washington State's Wiser Lake is a small, picturesque body of water just a few miles south of Lynden. When I designed the house, I wanted to create something that complemented the natural surrounding beauty and didn't try to compete with it. The Wiser Lake House takes advantage of natural materials that make sense in this setting: wood, glass, and metal. The rooms are understated, modern, and warm. We wanted to capture sweeping outdoor views throughout the home so we opted for large windows in the living spaces and many of the private areas, as well. There is a sense of openness and freedom when you are in the house, which I like to think of as an extension of the feeling you have while on the lake itself.

It was important that the rear exterior of the house offer plenty of outdoor living and entertainment space. What's the point of living on a lake if you can't enjoy the scenery? We created covered and uncovered patios for this reason. Here, the family can have dinner, host large gatherings, or just enjoy a quiet cup of coffee in the morning. The butterfly roof, strong lines, and deep overhangs add the perfect touch of drama to the design. Even though neighbors aren't far from the house, the property has a quiet sense of serenity because the backyard opens up directly to the water.
Photographs by Damian Vines Photography
Designed by CLT Design Build, Lynden, WA, page 215

Scan this QR code to view more custom homes designed by CLT Design Build

DAVID POOL ARCHITECTURE

Browns Point Residence, Browns Point, WA

BROWNS POINT RESIDENCE
Browns Point, WA

This home is a stunning architectural masterpiece nestled in a well-established residential neighborhood of Washington. The exceptional home effortlessly combines contemporary design with a warm and inviting atmosphere perfectly tailored to the unique aesthetics of the Pacific Northwest region. We skillfully leveraged the natural topography of the site, which boasted a striking grade differential, offering panoramic views of the Puget Sound and the majestic Olympic Mountains. Harnessing the power of natural daylight, the residence radiates an enchanting glow accentuated by the extensive use of Western red cedar on the exterior and the elegance of Douglas fir ceilings within.

Creating a seamless integration with the awe-inspiring natural surroundings, the architect incorporated expansive sliding glass door panels, forging a harmonious connection between indoor and outdoor spaces. At the heart of this remarkable abode lies the kitchen, a central organizing element that transcends its utilitarian purpose to become the primary social space. Local craftsmanship shines through the custom cabinetry and furniture, meticulously crafted from reclaimed elm slabs adorned with captivating live-edge detailing, courtesy of the talented artisans at Madera Furniture Company. Adding to the allure of the residence is the covered lower-level living space, providing a shaded sanctuary from the intense summer sun with a large, bi-folding, ,operable-glass wall system. The thoughtful planning and design of this house successfully enhance and complement the unique lifestyle of the homeowners, ensuring a truly personalized living experience that profoundly connects with nature.

Photographs by William Wright Photography
**Designed by David Pool Architecture,
Seattle/Tacoma, WA, page 215**

DONNALLY ARCHITECTS

Ship to Shore, Tulalip, WA

148 Inspired West Coast Homes

 *Scan this QR code to view more inspiring homes by Donnally Architects*

SHIP TO SHORE
Tulalip, WA

After a long and well-respected career captaining U.S. Navy ships and submarines, this homeowner and his wife retired onshore with the goal of looking back across the waters he had once sailed. This three-bedroom vacation home, nestled into the hillside about an hour north of Seattle, replaced a small block house on a waterfront lot held by his family for more than 100 years. The original plan was to do a modest renovation and addition, but once the project got going it became clear that a full rebuild would be necessary. The new home required an extensive coordination of complex shoreline setback requirements to find a solution that gave every living space a panoramic view of the water. A variety of open and covered outdoor spaces, including a picturesque dining gazebo, provide many opportunities to enjoy the waterfront views through the seasons. An avid DIYer, the homeowner has a nicely outfitted workshop hidden underneath the deck—he even completed most of the home's trim and finish-out, as well as all the electrical, himself. Now, the couple's children and grandchildren are able to visit often and continue the family tradition of treasuring this property.
Photographs by Sozinho Imagery
Designed by Donnally Architects, Seattle, WA, page 215

PAR TWO
Seattle, WA

The Seattle floating home community, limited now to the remaining 520 float slips, is among the largest in the world. With humble beginnings in the late nineteenth century, they have now become highly sought out for the unique opportunity they offer to live on the water in an urban environment. The diminishing number of those awaiting a major renovation makes them especially valuable. When this young couple bought the worst house on the dock, everyone was glad someone would finally replace the old eyesore. The husband had two non-negotiable requirements: a covered deck with a large, retractable window through which to watch sports on the living room TV, and a rooftop putting green to hone his short game. For her, extensive cabinetry and storage to put away daily items for a clutter-free environment was also a must. The design strategy arranged the personal spaces on the main level, where privacy was easier to control, and put the living spaces in a large open plan on the second level, where views to the city skyline and surrounding lake environs could be had across adjacent rooftops. Light-colored finishes and carefully placed windows provide a bright, contemporary interior. This house is one of more than a dozen floating home projects that we have designed.
Photographs by Sozinho Imagery
Designed by Donnally Architects, Seattle, WA, page 215

Scan this QR code to view a video showing the design of this floating home

FIRST LAMP ARCHITECTURE

Lake Tapps Getaway, Bonny Lake, WA

LAKE TAPPS GETAWAY
Bonney Lake, WA

Our homes are meant to be extraordinary, to make an impression on the people who live in them, visit them, and even see them from afar. Nestled on the shores of Lake Tapps, this home shows off the seamless harmony between architecture and environment as our design celebrates the beauty of its surroundings. The home's overarching concept revolves around its harmonious integration with a challenging, steep-slope hillside. A deliberate step-down approach accomplishes this and unveils captivating vistas of Lake Tapps and the majestic backdrop of Mount Rainier. Our design ethos extends to the windows themselves, as we aimed to mirror the elegance of the surrounding trees. The windows, characterized by their slender and lofty profiles, emulate the trunks of trees, while the sporadic mullions artfully evoke the intricate branching patterns you'd find in nature. To further anchor the structure in its environment, we employed a wealth of natural materials such as wood and concrete, ensuring a blend with the organic surroundings. One of the most compelling aspects of residential architecture is the unique ability of those who conceive the design to also bring it to life through construction. This dynamic process allows our projects to evolve organically, which you can get a clear sense of when you see this home. It has a natural essence to it, and nothing feels forced.

The lakeside perspective captures the dwelling's waterfront façade, which flows effortlessly into its surroundings. On the eastern side, you'll find slider window patterns that reflect nature, as well as a negative-edge pool. A panoramic vista of Lake Tapps is framed by a large sliding door so the lines of indoor and outdoor living become blurred. The living space

harmonizes organic and industrial elements for a modern yet warm ambience that make sense for a lakeside respite. We build homes to shape the daily lives and feelings of their residents and, because of that, we know our work is meaningful. The rooms aren't simply meant to function for life's most basic needs, but are intended to be contemplative, emotional, and stand as examples of the relationship between human ingenuity and the physical world.

The Lake Tapps residence is an example of how we breathe life into spaces, honoring the intricate dance between design and construction, and celebrating the profound influence of the built environment on the human spirit. We are guided by the unwavering belief that the pursuit of beauty, functionality, and sustainability is a noble endeavor that enriches lives, strengthens connections, and leaves an indelible mark on the tapestry of our shared existence.

Just as we create our surroundings and mold our spaces, our spaces in turn mold us. This reciprocity underscores the importance of my firm's work. I sincerely believe that our surroundings wield a remarkable power to influence our lives, emotions, and experiences. That's why the interior of the homes I design are so important—I know the impact it will have on the families. We worked with the Seattle-based firm Mandy Callaway Interiors for the Lake Tapps Getaway. Her balanced, understated approach added to the home's timeless style.

Interior design by Mandy Callaway Interiors
Photographs by Tim Bies Photography
Architecture designed by First Lamp Architects, Seattle, WA, page 215

ISLAND ARCHITECTURE
KAPLAN HOMES

Blakely Island A-Frame, Washington

BLAKELY ISLAND A-FRAME
Anacortes, WA

The original A-frame was built in 1965 by the owner's father, who was a pilot and used the hangar next door. It had fallen into disuse and disrepair, and demolition was even discussed, but ultimately the home is full of childhood memories and sentimental value. The house faces the community's small-airplane runway, and watching planes land and take off is the main entertainment during the summer months. Therefore it felt only natural for architect Nina LeBaron to add "airplane wings," a solution to gain space and form a connection to the A-frame in a unique way. One "wing" contains a proper dining room with an outdoor seating area and fire pit, while the other houses the primary bedroom suite with its own private deck. A proper staircase was added to gain access to the loft, replacing a steep, narrow ladder. Builder Nate Kaplan actually cut the top half of the A-frame off and suspended it while windows and LaCantina doors were framed. Blakely Island is a part of the San Juan Islands and therefore only accessible by private plane or boat, so all materials and equipment had to be specially barged in from the mainland, and the crew moved into the hangar during the week.
Photographs courtesy of Island Architecture & Kaplan Homes
Designed by Island Architecture & Kaplan Homes, Anacortes, WA, page 215

MACPHERSON CONSTRUCTION & DESIGN

Lakeside Retreat, Hunts Point, WA

166 Inspired West Coast Homes

Scan this QR code to view a video tour of this magnificent waterfront home

LAKESIDE RETREAT
Hunts Point, WA

Located in the exclusive high-end neighborhood of Hunts Point, on one of the last undeveloped lots in the neighborhood, this home required a creative approach to meet specific zoning requirements. Every jurisdiction has unique codes related to lot coverage and building heights, and this project was no exception. The home and landscaping have been carved into the site so that it responds to the natural topography. Utilizing curved roofs to maximize the volume within the side setbacks, the roofs and wood ceilings create a comfortable enclosure inside the home. Curved glulam beams beautifully frame the custom lighting within. Full-height windows bring in light and views of Lake Washington, and large sliding doors provide connection between interior and exterior spaces. The use of steel, stone, and stucco blend in with the natural surroundings and sooth the senses, capturing the visual and tactile properties of the materials. The interior design—thanks to senior interior designer Kathy Blethen—complements the materials without overpowering the spaces. Our integration of the pool and landscape acknowledges the topography and make seamless transitions between the interior and exterior, no matter what the day brings.

Photographs by Clarity Northwest, Bobby Erdt

Designed by MacPherson Construction & Design, Sammamish, WA, page 215

EVERGREEN POINT MODERN
Medina, WA

The Medina Modern Residence stands as an example of pure luxury. You'll see that contemporary design flourishes here amidst an aura of refinement. Located high above Lake Washington, this home showcases a covered patio, pool and spa, fire pit, and sport court, linking the outdoor activity spaces with the active zones of the home. These exterior features, combined with the interior open spaces, create a true entertaining mecca. Our design team accomplished these connections with floor-to-ceiling openings that bathe the interior in an abundance of natural light. The exterior finishes were kept simple and clean to allow the interior to shine. This exclusive residence boasts impeccable craftsmanship, beautifully complemented by sophisticated screen accents that add a touch of allure to its modern interiors. Finishes, furniture, and fixtures were all carefully selected to stand out and make a visual statement, so that each space is aesthetically distinct.

Photographs by Ben Benschneider
Designed by MacPherson Construction & Design, Sammamish, WA, page 215

Scan this QR code to view a video tour of this magnificent home

NEWPORT SHORES FARMHOUSE
Newport Shores, Bellevue, WA

Situated on the canals of Bellevue with direct access to the waters of Lake Washington, this Newport Shores modern farmhouse addresses the concept of spatial volume and verticality. This is the second new-home project for this wonderful family. A mix of exterior geometric volumes evokes how a farmhouse may have grown over the years of its life. The cheery, bright white board and batten siding is softened by the masses of warmth coming from the natural stone facades. Through our creativity, we reveal how natural light can elevate the living experience for the owners in a simplified space. The home is expressly designed for the client's lifestyle and individual family needs. Large social interaction areas mixed with getaway spaces assure a place for every mood. The design of the home creates a sense of warmth and softness through the materiality of the custom interiors and blurs the threshold of inside and outside for exceptional outdoor living and entertaining.
Photographs by Ben Benschneider
Designed by MacPherson Construction & Design, Sammamish, WA, page 215

Scan this QR code to view more amazing projects from MacPherson Construction

British Columbia Homes

Architecture in British Columbia, particularly in Vancouver, reflects a unique blend of urban innovation and natural integration. Known as the City of Glass, Vancouver's skyline has been dominated for decades by glass high-rises, both commercial and residential. However, recent iconic structures—such as Vancouver House by Bjarke Ingels, The Cardero by Henriquez Architects, and Alberni Tower by Kengo Kuma—are redefining this narrative with their postmodern philosophy and aesthetics.

In the suburbs and the British Columbia interior, residential design showcases an eclectic mix of styles. You'll find American Craftsman, California Bungalow, Dingbat, and the infamous Vancouver Special, gabled homes with a box-like appearance. Contemporary designs often reinterpret these influences or draw inspiration from West Coast Modernism, initially popularized by Arthur Erickson, Ned Pratt, and B.C. Binning after World War II. This style beautifully integrates the region's abundant nature with indoor living through plentiful overhangs, large windows, open floor plans, and custom-built features that utilize natural materials and sustainable practices.

In British Columbia, design elements often emphasize a strong connection to the surrounding landscape. Features such as expansive windows for natural light and breathtaking views, open spaces that encourage flow between indoors and outdoors, and the use of local materials are prevalent. Additionally, there's a focus on sustainability and environmentally-friendly practices, reflecting a commitment to preserving the region's natural beauty.

The cultural diversity also enriches our projects, bringing depth and perspective to our designs. My team speaks over a dozen languages, fostering an inclusive atmosphere that values kindness and respect. The most rewarding part of my work is transforming living and working spaces into interactive environments where occupants connect with each other and their surroundings, fostering a welcoming atmosphere that meets their needs and aspirations. The homes you see featured in this chapter offer just a glimpse into the dynamics of the region.

Mila Djuras
Intermind Design, Inc.
New Westminster, BC
see page 216

CARA INTERIORS

West Coast With A Twist, White Rock, BC

WEST COAST WITH A TWIST
White Rock, BC

Regardless of the project, practical issues inform the overall design of a room. This was certainly the case for our clients who dreamt of a kitchen that was modern, warm, and would wow guests. We achieved this look, but not without a few difficulties to overcome along the way. In the kitchen, there were structural drops that housed HVAC and beams that could not be moved, causing us to create a complex design which worked beautifully for the space. In addition, we used our creativity with the lighting due to the kitchen's vaulted ceiling and three skylights. Track lighting and elegant LED drop pendants proved the ideal solution. In an effort to create more storage, we extended the north wall. In the original plan, the powder room was in an open area off the kitchen, which created an awkward feeling for guests using the washroom. The extension of the north kitchen wall solved this problem while providing additional storage.

The principal ensuite originally had two levels where the shower dropped down 12 inches, which was a poor use of space. We changed the design by raising the floor to one level, allowing for a European wet room-inspired space. The tile needed to have a dramatic effect to coordinate with the other areas of the home, therefore we chose charcoal 24-by-48 tiles placed vertically, creating a herringbone look with their natural texture.

Photographs by Julian Plimley Photography

Designed by Cara Interiors, Surrey, BC, page 216

DCYT ARCHITECTURE

Vancouver Contemporary, Burnaby, BC

VANCOUVER CONTEMPORARY
Burnaby, BC

Far from your typical single-family home, this Vancouver residence is designed with separate living quarters to accommodate three families and three generations, all under one roof. By splitting the house into multiple levels and creating side-by-side spaces, the design intends to create privacy between families and yet still maintain open and welcoming communal areas where everyone in the family could gather.

The ground level of this custom house is designed as a communal space with a shared living room, dining room, and kitchen, while a separate suite is also strategically placed on this level for the grandparent who may be challenged with mobility in the coming years. The upper floors are split into half levels, with each level housing one of the two co-owners and families separately. The concept of split-levels helps provide the notion of privacy for each family but at the same time, because of its proximity, reinforces the togetherness of the two families. The lower level is designed to be a totally separate and self-contained rental suite for yet another family.

The exterior of the house is cladded with articulating metal sidings and panels instead of natural wood sidings because of longevity and maintenance concerns. With the intention to relate this contemporary West Coast home to its context, horizontal aluminum siding with a traditional faux wood finish is chosen to wrap around the first level of the house. In contrast, the second level is cladded with standing-seam metal panels which extend up the roof to form a seamless and contemporary architectural element. The concept of mixing the traditional and contemporary elements on the architectural expression serves as a reflection of the different generations residing harmoniously within.

Photographs by Upper Left Photography / Janet Mak / Douglas Cheung
Designed by DCYT Architecture, Vancouver, BC, page 216

HYNESITE DESIGNS

West Vancouver Beach House, West Vancouver, BC

WEST VANCOUVER BEACH HOUSE
West Vancouver, BC

Great design is balanced proportions and flow of space with careful selection of colors and material, and when you hit that sweet spot, it just feels right. That was certainly the case for the West Vancouver Beach House. Built by Kerr Construction, the custom design-and-build project reveals careful attention to even the tiniest detail. We achieved a warm yet open feel with a double-sided, indoor-outdoor fireplace and folding, sliding doors. It makes the living space contiguous with the outdoors to create an ideal entertaining space. I like to pull in elements of a home's site and natural surroundings, which I did here with subtle interior design details and finishes that mimic the nearby water and beach. You'll find details such as the 350-million-year-old seabed fossils mounted above the stone fireplace, the primary bathroom tiles that give the impression of shimmering sand under your feet, and the suspended fishing net chandelier above the primary bathroom tub dripping with crystal 'water' drops. Combining bleached oak flooring with the dark walnut staircase handrails creates visually dramatic, sweeping lines along with a sea-inspired art installation on the curved wall of the staircase. Continuing the cohesive flow of the details throughout the home, rich walnut accents and tonally soft, bleached-oak, wide-plank flooring smoothly blend with natural materials such as salt stone backsplashes and Bianco Chateau quartzite countertops to achieve the nature-inspired look.

Photographs by Martin Knowles Photography
Designed by Hynesite Designs, Vancouver, BC, page 216

En Garde, Vancouver BC

INTERMIND DESIGN, INC.

EN GARDE
Vancouver, BC

There was no shortage of challenges to overcome during the renovation of this 1980s penthouse. Overall, it was poorly designed with limited floor-to-ceiling window openings and no air conditioning, which made for an unbearable living space. The homeowners have strong ties to Olympic fencing and are a blended family with grown children. They knew this would be their last big investment, and we wanted to make it completely customized to their lifestyles. We used smart design to create a stunning makeover including their dream primary suite, a spacious and functional kitchen, offices, and details that you'd expect to see in a luxury penthouse. Hand-curated, exquisite finishes seamlessly blend with built-ins, adding architectural interest. We included an energy efficient, custom-built fireplace that allows for a full-gas stove, and a new air-conditioning system. The high-end, high-performance Energy Star appliances include a small-appliance pull-out cabinet, Sub-Zero 16-inch wine fridge, and built-in recycling and compost pull-outs, making the kitchen a dream for any host. We installed window film to block 90 percent of UV and infrared light, and 80 percent of the solar heat that would otherwise come through.
Photographs by Keith Henderson
**Designed by Intermind Design, Inc.,
New Westminster, BC, page 216**

PROFICIENCY
Vancouver, BC

We had the pleasure of embarking on a significant project located in the heart of Vancouver's West Side for a professional couple. After two-and-a-half decades abroad, they yearned to return to Vancouver, and in the process purchased an as-is spec house that had been uninhabited for quite some time. From purchasing through design and construction, the entire process was coordinated virtually. The scope of work was expansive and involved a complete rebirth of the interior, with an emphasis on creating a spacious, open floorplan throughout. The newly whitewashed exterior was enriched with a custom-stained front door, modern black windows, and doors that fully extend off the kitchen onto a vast deck. Upgrades such as a new HVAC system, re-piping, rewiring, and sound and alarm systems all contribute to the amazing transformation.

The layout enhancements became the backdrop for design innovation, giving life to platforms, ceiling drops, built-ins, decorative wall paneling, and vision brought to life, including the artistically waved spiral staircase. The interior speaks a language of refinement and elegance, blending high-end luxury with the relaxed spirit of the West Coast. Wide-plank white oak graces the floors, Herrera marble adorns the surfaces, custom lighting fixtures cast their glow, and striking wall murals narrate stories of travel adventures near and far. The house now truly reflects the couple's spirited journey through life. A home, designed for them, in the city they had missed.

Photographs by Keith Henderson

Designed by Intermind Design, Inc., New Westminster, BC, page 216

BOHEMIAN BLUE
Vancouver, BC

We created an ideal home for people who love to entertain and cook. These homeowners are free-spirited empty nesters who wanted a Bohemian-style, open-plan design with a spacious living room, dining room, and kitchen, plus expansive storage and counter space. Top-of-the-line appliances include an eye-catching, professional, 36-inch red gas range with a write-on hood, plus a wine fridge and dishwasher. In the dining room, the oval Carrara-top dining table fuses the open plan and shows off rich blue-black, velvet-textured chairs. We found creative solutions for a number of construction challenges through innovative yet budget-saving reconfiguration of the rooms. The house originally had a wide, dysfunctional layout, but we created a floorplan that made sense for them, including the luxury primary suite. The ensuite's chandelier complements striped floor-to-ceiling Striata tiles and baby-blue glass mosaic tiles that give the bathroom a unique, personalized look. We also added a concrete-like laminate vanity, a stand-alone shower, heated tiles, and undermount lighting with six settings to help soothe the homeowners after a long day. The project came in 10 percent under the budget and two weeks before our estimated finish date, which is something we are proud of. We always work to deliver those kinds of results to homeowners.

Photographs by Keith Henderson

**Designed by Intermind Design, Inc.,
New Westminster, BC, page 216**

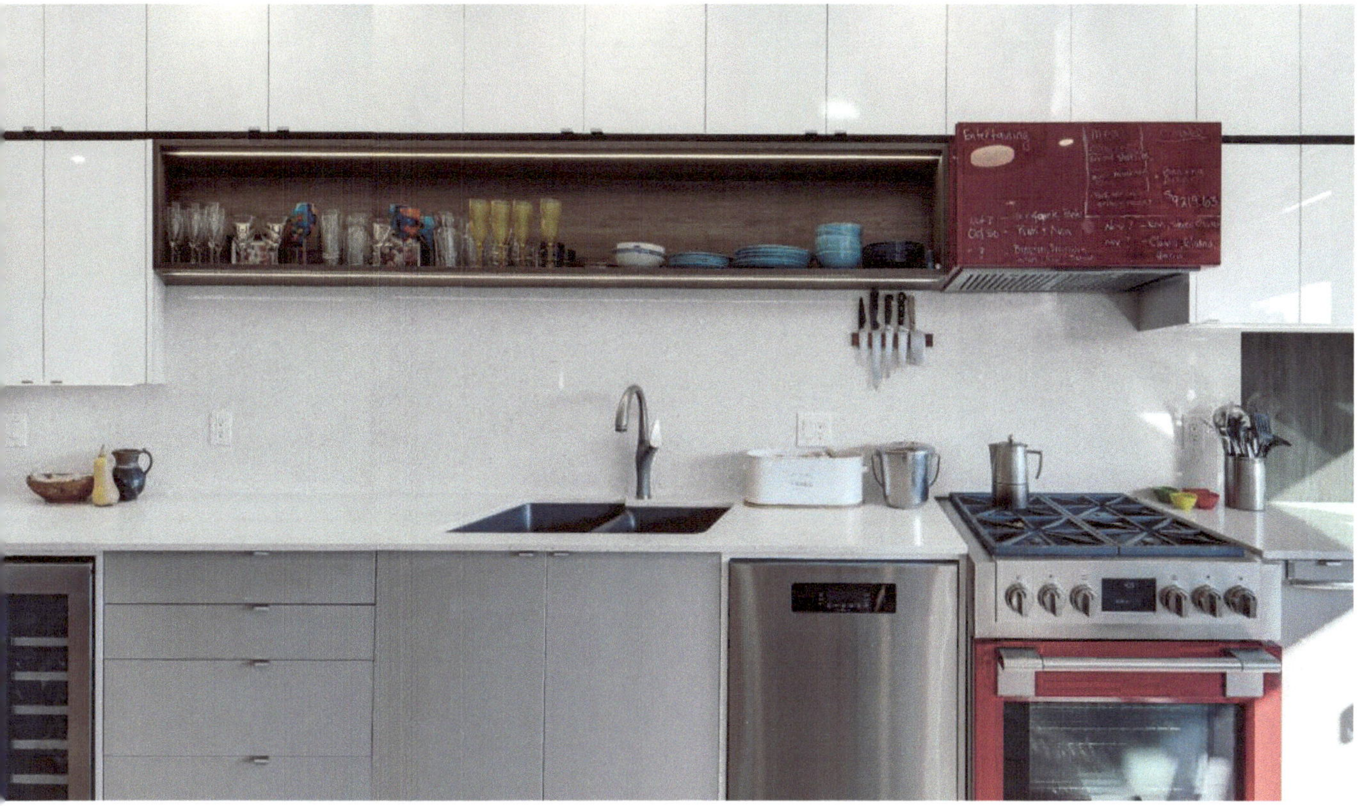

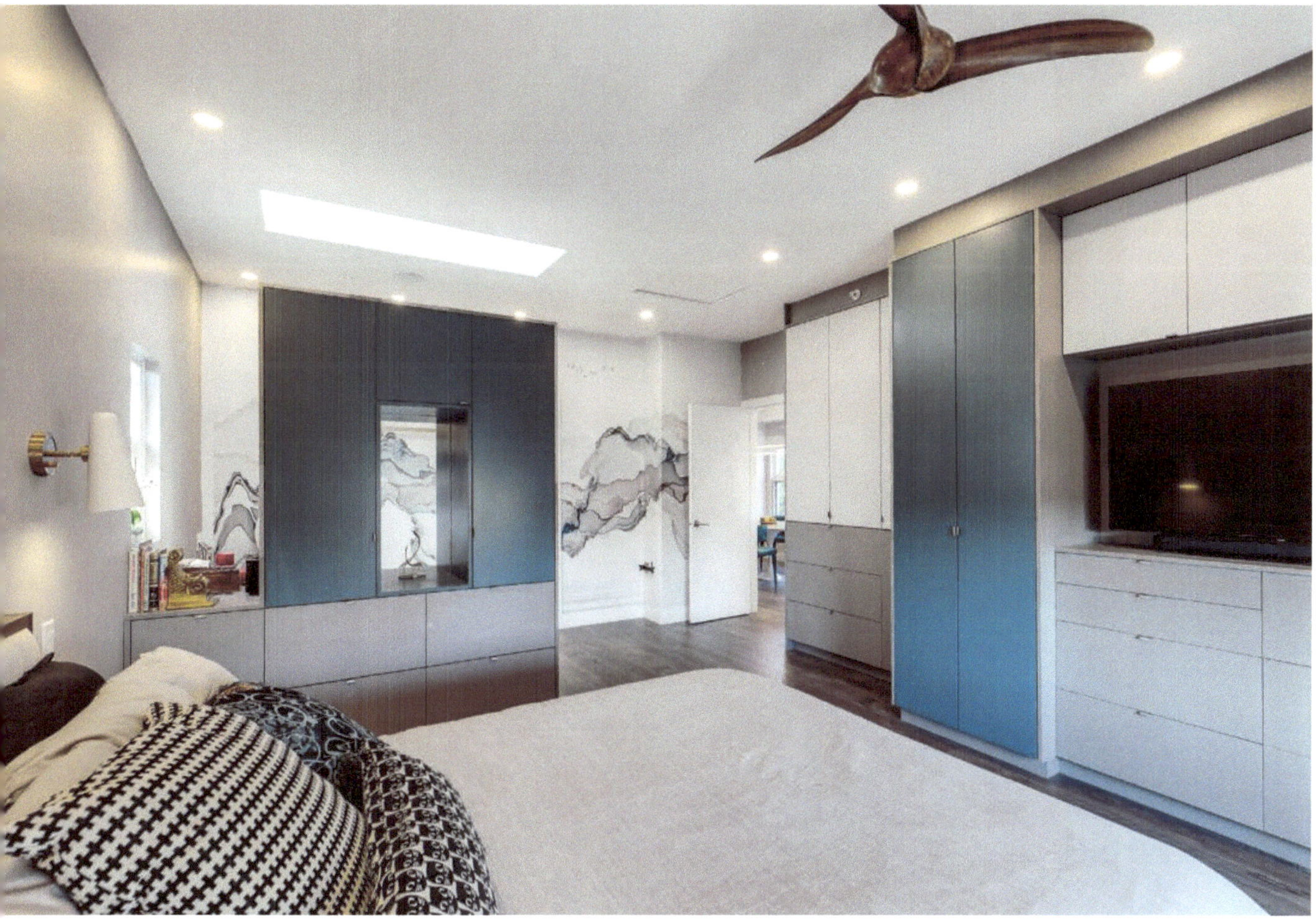

LITERARI
North Vancouver, BC

Literari was a complex renovation where I feel we mastered spatial planning. Throughout the space we used large windows for ample natural light and to bring the splendid foliage of Lynn Valley indoors. We maximized the openness of the home while distinctively defining spaces with multiple stairways, geometric vaulted-and-beamed ceilings, and full-size glass walls. Built-in units are concealed in textured light wood luxury finishes and concrete-inspired surfaces. Matching light wood flooring grounds the honed Ceppo Di Gre marble wrapped around the corner wood-burning fireplace. Heavy, transparent acrylic Z chairs sit around a custom cantilevered glass table with a multi-coat finish in gold, copper, and silver—built by the client's husband. The double waterfall catches the eye with its high backsplash in gold, white, and grey. And in the cozy reading corner, rattan armchairs and a Frida Kahlo blanket warm the space. The contemporary, landscape-inspired paintings reflect the spirit of the Pacific Northwest, while displayed artifacts—African tribal masks, colorful glass, and artistic pottery—connect time and space. Like all renovations that we undertake, working closely with clients is my favorite part of the project. In this particular project, creating the space felt like orchestrating an intellectual, sensory, and spiritual portrait of an exceptional woman surrounded by the family she adores.

Photographs by Keith Henderson

Designed by Intermind Design, Inc., New Westminster, BC, page 216

ISOMETRIX DESIGN INC.

Alberni Penthouse, Vancouver BC

ALBERNI PENTHOUSE
Vancouver, BC

The challenge that many interior designers face is to take a space and make it feel like a million dollars, for a lot less. This was the challenge we had with the Alberni Penthouse.

This 3,000-square-foot penthouse duplex is situated in downtown Vancouver and enjoys stunning ocean and mountain views. The building's circular shape and location inspired the owner to request a yacht-themed aesthetic for the home, which is evident throughout. Stainless-steel portholes were inserted into some of the doors and the circular hallway rotunda conjures up a nautical compass idea. Though after careful thought and with budget in mind, an abstract version was custom designed using waterjet sawn porcelain tiles. "Teak and holly" floors were originally requested but due to the prohibitively high costs, grey oak was substituted and worked nicely.

Up the spiral staircase we enter the mezzanine level, which was completely rearranged. The main kitchen/dining area was moved upstairs to take advantage of the fantastic panoramic mountain and ocean views and wrap-around patio. A carefully crafted circular kitchen was designed to mimic the curved building's envelope. Another feature of this unit was the architectural void in the floor upstairs. Engineers were consulted to see if the void could safely be covered with thick glass, thereby gaining floor space but maintaining the integrity of the architecture. It turned out to be a great success, and color-changing LED strip lights were installed underneath to give it a dramatic glow at night.
Photographs by Ema Peters
Designed by Isometrix Design Inc., Vancouver, BC, page 216

STEP ONE DESIGN

Riviera Escape, Victoria, BC

RIVIERA ESCAPE
Victoria, BC

Inspired by abstract design, the Riviera Escape achieves the more intense, modern West Coast aesthetic that we wanted. We chose multi-pitched sloping roofs, contrasting white stucco with dark siding, natural stone veneer, and tall solid timber columns with braces. Inside, the ceilings soar thanks to the framing of the multi-pitched roof and the result is a dramatic, airy interior. There are steel stairs and an open media loft that looks down into the entryway and living room. At more than 3,500 square feet, the design includes a luxurious primary suite and two upstairs bedrooms. Throughout the home, you'll notice touches of Scandinavian design elements combined with natural finishes and materials like wood and metal, giving a nature-inspired feel to the rooms.

Obviously, with a natural surrounding as beautiful as this, we wanted to include as much of the outside environment into the home as possible. We made the floorplan angular, with sharp extending lines that make sense for the home's lot. The builder, Designated Developments, executed this design perfectly. The angles help open up the exterior views and invite outdoor living. It's impossible to stand in the house and not notice the stunning, lush natural landscape. For added curb appeal, an L-shaped, three-car garage creates a welcoming courtyard as you approach the home and reduces the emphasis on the garage doors that face the street.
Photographs by Jacob McNeil
Designed by Step One Design, Victoria, BC, page 216

Scan this QR code to view more custom homes designed by Step One Design..

MANSION ON THE GREEN
Langford, BC

Tucked in the picturesque neighborhood of Bear Mountain with a surrounding golf course, we created a traditional, manor-style home that offers luxury living and timeless beauty. In the distance, you can see views of Mount Finlayson and lush, rolling terrain. Because of the land's beauty, we included an outdoor living space that looks directly onto the golf course fairway. The homeowner wanted the rear of the home to have a stunning aesthetic so we made the ceiling large, vaulted, and eye-catching. I incorporated flat roofs and some surprising elements into the traditional steep pitches to give the home visual interest.

Perfect for hosting family and friends, the floorplan allows for tons of natural light and a kitchen that would make any chef envious. It includes high-tech appliances, a large prep area, and flows beautifully into the dining and living spaces. Our design of the manor spared no detail. Grateful acknowledgement to the builder, Shane Hughes Construction, for their attention and execution of our designs.. The primary suite includes a number of high-end touches in its serene and spa-like bathroom, the carefully crafted woodwork, and roomy closet. For the homeowners, it's the ideal respite to get away from it all at the end of the day.

Photographs by Jody Beck
Designed by Step One Design, Victoria, BC, page 216

450 Parc, Kelowna, BC

VINEYARD DEVELOPMENTS

450 PARC
Kelowna, BC

Architectural brilliance, sophisticated living, and a singular design—these traits are reflected in 450 Parc, a luxury real estate community that stands out from its contemporaries. It's no surprise that the homes were quickly claimed, as each residence offers the privacy and spaciousness of a single-family home with its own unique appeal. Convenience abounds, as 450 Parc boasts all of the perks and amenities of an upscale condominium community. The homes are occupied by owners and it includes an impressive private lobby with a semi-private elevator.

We wanted the past and present to coexist harmoniously, resulting in a building that stands as a testament to timeless design and architectural innovation. Akin to the timeless architecture found in old-town Manhattan, 450 Parc marries Old-World charm and contemporary aesthetics. But it's not just about beauty. We integrated a deep connection with nature into the design, which is a hallmark of the luxurious Okanagan lifestyle. Each residence offers expansive views of the nearby park and, for many, breathtaking vistas of Okanagan Lake. The thoughtful orientation of the homes allows for sun-drenched patios, ensuring a seamless integration of indoor and outdoor living spaces. It's ideal for those moments of relaxation and entertainment.

450 Parc is a manifestation of luxury, elegance, and modern sophistication that promises an unrivalled living experience in Kelowna's most sought-after neighborhood. For those seeking to transition to a carefree, luxury lifestyle without compromise, 450 Parc presents an unprecedented opportunity to live in a home that is as unique as the individuals it welcomes.

Photographs by Colin Jewall Photography
Designed by Vineyard Developments, Kelowna, BC, page 216

211

Meet the Designers
SOUTHERN CALIFORNIA

(fer) studio - see pages 14-17

Christopher Mercier, AIA
1159 East Hyde Park Boulevard
Inglewood, CA 90302
310.672.4749
ferstudio.com

Christopher L. Mercier is the president and founder of (fer) studio, or form - environment - research, an interdisciplinary architecture and urban design firm. The core philosophy driving their work revolves around creating highly individualized environments, carefully crafted to enhance and elevate how people live, experience, think, and move in the world. Raised in Michigan, Christopher developed an early and ongoing inquiry around the relationship between architecture, the visual arts, and the physical environment. Today, he leverages this background, coupled with more than 30 years of professional expertise and a creative dynamic (fer) studio team, to advance the mission of improving human experience/performance through the daily and deliberate practice of form, environment, and research.

Amit Apel Design Inc. - see pages 18-21

Amit Apel
33202 ¼ U Mulholland Highway
Malibu, CA 90265
310.317.0500
apeldesign.com

Although Malibu-based Amit Apel Design Inc. specializes in creating unique luxury homes, the development studio does so much more. Led by the gifted artist, innovator, and CEO Amit Apel, the firm has designed and built specialty concepts and hospitality projects across Europe, Asia, South America, and the United States. Additionally, Amit creates art, furniture, and a specialty line of products. His portfolio boasts 700-plus projects and an impressive list of high-profile clients that seek the firm's expertise and creativity. The team's innovative architecture and concepts challenge traditional ideas and forms, giving clients sustainable spaces that optimize the way people live.

Dean Larkin Design - see pages 22-29

Dean Larkin, AIA
8912 Hollywood Hills Road
Los Angeles, CA 90046
323.654.7500
deanlarkindesign.com

Architecture is such a passion and a way of life for Dean Larkin that he didn't so much choose it as a career—it chose him. He graduated from the renowned University of Southern California's School of Architecture and became the first employee of Richard Landry, founder of Landry Design Group. While there, Dean worked on numerous high-end residential and upscale destination projects around the world. He opened his namesake firm, in 1999 with a focus on high-end private residences that capture the essence of Southern California, balancing luxury with casual elegance. Dean's emphasis on livable glamour has been fueling stunning modern designs under Dean Larkin Design ever since.

Dworsky Architecture - see pages 30-37

Douglas Dworsky
1405 Woodruff Avenue
Los Angeles, CA 90024
310.441.1211
dworskyarchitecture.com

Doug Dworsky's passion for architecture developed at an early age. His father was also an architect and Doug grew up touring construction sites and studying design models with him. That early inspiration led him to study architecture at Princeton and Yale, where he graduated Summa Cum Laude and Phi Beta Kappa among other honors, eventually opening his own firm. Over the years, Doug has acquired experience in institutional, commercial, and residential architecture. In his residential architectural design, Doug strives to develop a design vocabulary that is modern, timeless, and spacious, creating living environments that are warm, inviting, and intimate. His architectural work has been published in national and international architectural journals and honored by national and local architectural design award programs.

Elyssa Contardo Interior Design - see pages 38-41

Elyssa Contardo
74020 Alessandro Drive, Suite F
Palm Desert, CA 92260
760.579.8113
elyssacontardo.com

Known for creating rich, inspired spaces, Elyssa Contardo approaches her residential work with sophisticated creativity and the discipline of a seasoned project manager. Her interiors simultaneously evoke the opulence of bygone eras while remaining grounded in the organic materiality of the region. Honed through years of experience, Elyssa's discerning eye for detail adds a warm and elevated touch to both new builds and turnkey properties. With a history of successful projects varying in scale, scope, and budget, Elyssa integrates each client's intrinsic needs with their unique spirit, creating unparalleled, extraordinary spaces.

JF Carlson Architects - see pages 42-45

JF Carlson Architects
2300 Cliff Drive
Newport Beach, CA. 92663
949.645.3051
jfcarlsonarchitects.com

As an architect in California for more than 40 years, Jim Carlson knows how to deliver dream homes to clients all over Southern California. As the principal of his firm, Jim does all the heavy lifting on projects: design, coordination, and entitlement work. The boutique firm is highly adept at hands-on project management and offers an array of design services. With every home, remodel, or renovation, Jim works to get to know the homeowners personally so he can act as a conduit between them and their dream home. His goal is always to provide the design that meets the owners' style, needs, and features while exceeding their expectations.

RLB Architecture - see pages 46-53

Richard Blumenberg, AIA, LEED AP
15200 Sunset Boulevard, Suite 200
Pacific Palisades, CA 90272
310.459.0244
rlbarchitecture.com

Richard Blumenberg has one goal: to create beautiful, luxurious, and functional homes for his clients while acting as their trusted guide through each step of the process. A native Angeleno, Blumenberg founded his own firm in 1997, building on 20 years of accumulated experience before that to now primarily focus on new-home builds, remodels, additions, and spec houses. A passionate architect with a deep appreciation for quality and craftsmanship, he draws his inspiration from traditional architectural styles of the past, yet always stays mindful of the demands of the present and keeps a keen eye trained toward the future.

Sheila Todd Interiors - see pages 54-57

Sheila Todd
Pacific Palisades, CA 90272
design@sheilatoddinteriors.com
@sheilatoddinteriors
sheilatoddinteriors.com

Sheila Todd's background in the fashion industry gives her a unique eye for interior design. After studying at New York City's Parson's School of Design, Sheila spent 25 years designing footwear and accessories for a number of modern brands. As she traveled the world, her passion for interior architecture and decorative painting was ignited, resulting in her namesake firm. Sheila has extensive experience in reconstruction, kitchen and bathroom design, all-interior and exterior detailing, decorating, and final staging. Working with a range of clients from New York to California, Sheila Todd Interiors offers a soft, contemporary approach to timeless coastal design.

NORTHERN CALIFORNIA

BLAINE Architects - *see pages* 60-63

Megan Blaine, AIA
Keith Blaine, AIA, LEED BD+C
San Jose, CA 95112
408.890.8800
blainearchitects.com

Partners in life and business, Megan and Keith Blaine met at the AIA National convention in 2006. They founded BLAINE architects in 2015 after working at Foster + Partners in London and Silicon Valley. Megan began her career in 2002, designing projects that ranged from high-end custom homes to Boulder's shelter for the homeless. From there, she designed multidisciplinary projects worldwide with an emphasis in high-end resort design. Keith received his architecture degree from USC and then worked in healthcare and education before joining Foster + Partners. Today, their studio tackles projects all over the West Coast, designing honest architecture that not only looks beautiful, but feels right.

Joseph Farrell Architecture - *see pages* 72-75

Joseph Farrell
1 Commercial Boulevard, Suite 106
Novato, CA 94949
415.884.2860
Farrellarc.com

Joseph Farrell Architecture's portfolio shows off a wide range of projects, however the soul of the firm is residential architecture. Founded in 1995, Joseph Farrell's firm was launched as a close-knit, three-person team focusing on the creation of artful homes that are energy-efficient and environmentally sensitive. His designs strive to integrate natural light, air, views, landscape, and community. The firm's portfolio includes luxury homes, remodels, vacation homes, and wineries.

DiVittorio Construction, Inc. - *see pages* 64-67

Roy DiVittorio
Campbell, CA 95008
408.655.0570
divittorioconstruction.com

Owner and founder of DiVittorio Construction, Inc., Roy DiVittorio prides himself on the relationships he's developed in his industry since beginning the family-owned company in 1986. Roy and his team prioritize honesty, integrity, and commitment with each project, and it's given them a trusted name in the Bay Area and beyond. The DiVittorio Construction team has created long-lasting connections with architects, Realtors, interior designers, sub-contractors, clients, respected vendors, and, of course, homeowners. Clients will find high standards, quality work, and top-notch safety practices. The firm mainly focuses as a specialty company in residential remodels, home additions, and new construction.

JTM Interiors - *see pages* 64-67

Janet Marena
San Jose, CA 95120
857.205.3062
jtminteriors.com

Janet Tosi Marena, owner and founder of JTM Interiors, sees her firm as more than simply a design business. Along with her close-knit team, Janet uses evidence-based design to build spaces that support health and well-being. Janet and her team are available throughout the entire project as they guide homeowners through the process of creation, from design to construction and to the procurement of art and accessories. Janet believes it's important to collaborate with the design team early in the process so you can maximize each professional's talents and opinions. It helps ensure that the team will ultimately bring the homeowners' vision to life.

DiVittorio Designs LLC - *see pages* 64-67

Danielle DiVittorio Malloy
San Jose, CA 95125
408.655.0565
divittoriodesigns.com

Growing up in the construction industry, Danielle DiVittorio Malloy, owner and founder of DiVittorio Designs LLC, is no stranger to understanding what it takes to design a forever home. DiVittorio Designs is grounded in the practice of dedication, collaboration, and customization, translating into functional designed spaces. Danielle emphasizes running a business that places her client's needs and wants in the critical framework of building, structure, and systems. She believes the homeowner is the heart behind the architecture and by valuing each client relationship, Danielle has succeeded in generating residential design.

Mahya Salehi Studio - *see pages* 76-79

Mahya Salehi
1425 Treat Boulevard
Walnut Creek, CA 94596
510.631.4680
mahyasalehistudio.com

Mahya Salehi Studios is a full-service design firm located in the Bay Area. Owned and operated by architect and founder Mahya Salehi, the multi-disciplinary team of architects, interior designers, and visual artists work on projects ranging from single-family custom homes to boutique commercial spaces and educational facilities. By implementing a holistic approach to spatial design, the studio plans and manages the project roadmap from start to finish, with no detail left unnoticed. Through this intimate design journey, functional and responsive spaces are conceived and enriched with sophisticated and personable interiors. The studio's design approach combines functionality, aesthetics, and sustainability to create stunning, practical spaces.

DNM Architecture - *see pages* 68-71

David Marlatt
1A Gate 5 Road
Sausalito, CA 94645
415.348.8910
dnmarchitecture.com

If owner and founder David Marlatt had to find one commonality in his projects over the last 25 years, it would likely be that he and his team have placed the practical needs of clients and their communities first. He follows no set style, but instead seeks to solve design problems for clients as they arise. The role of the firm is to facilitate people as they navigate their environment and use buildings and homes for whatever purposes they are suited. David defines himself as a humanist and takes great pride in helping clients along their residential path.

Marc Newman Architect - *see pages* 80-83

Marc Newman
Oakland, CA 94611
510.508.5666
newmanarchitect.com

Marc Newman believes that designing and building should be done with care and intention, which is why his projects focus on the importance of sustainability. Marc brings more than 20 years of experience to his namesake firm, which has become known for its exceptional design, as well as strategies centered on sustainability. The Bay Area firm primarily creates single-family homes and Marc enjoys the personal relationship he builds with the homeowners. He's also worked on a number of award-winning project types including churches, schools, office buildings, fire stations, parks, live-work spaces, and community centers.

Mark Horton / Architecture - see pages 84-91

Mark Horton, FAIA
135 South Park
San Francisco, CA 94107
415.543.3347
mh-a.com

Mark Horton / Architecture begins each project with the understanding that the questions which should be asked are more important than knowing the presumed final answers. The solutions will come at the end of a true design process, but only if the correct questions are developed at the start. Founded in 1987 and licensed in both California and New York, MH/A truly believes that lives can be positively affected by design. The task for MH/A is to discover the point in space where the disparate arcs of desires and constraints coincide to reveal great design.

ORR Design Office - see pages 92-101

Gary Orr
East Bay & Sacramento
925.587.4200
916.441.4500
orrdreamhouse.com

Since 1995, the ORR Design Office has applied its trademarked Whole-Vision Design Process™ to the design of luxury custom homes, ranch estates, and memorable wineries. This unique approach fuses the firm's award-winning talents as both architects and landscape architects to transform everyday designs into personalized places that are extraordinary. Led by high-energy creative zealot Gary Orr, the office focuses on projects throughout the Bay Area, Wine Country, Sacramento Valley, and the Sierra Foothills. Gary says, "Our clients are young-at-heart dreamers, demanding perfectionists, and bold thinkers who are resolute individualists. They are craving unique places that will amplify and transform their lives—visionary spaces where the interior, exterior, and the site all seamlessly connect."

Saikley Architects - see pages 102-111

Alexandra Saikley
2533 Clement Avenue
Alameda, CA 94501
510.407.0413
saikleyarchitects.com

Led by principal architect Alexandra Saikley, Saikley Architects is a boutique San Francisco Bay Area firm with a simple philosophy: to make beautiful spaces. Always ready to solve multi-faceted challenges, Alexandra brings 30 years of experience to her trade and focuses on creating homes that make sense for her clients, the community, and the environment as a whole. Before founding the firm, Alexandra worked on a wide variety of projects, including live-work spaces, multi-unit housing, childcare centers, schools, churches, and hospitals. Today, Saikley Architects has designed more than 350 homes in the Bay Area.

OREGON

Nordby Design, Architecture & Interiors - see pages 112-119

Jon and Julie Nordby
16148 Boones Ferry Road
Lake Oswego, OR 97035
503.305.6426
www.Nordby.design

Run by husband-and-wife team Jon and Julie Nordby, Nordby Design began more than 22 years ago with a passion for architecture, design, innovation, and the desire to give people their dream homes. With 40-plus years in the industry, Jon runs the architectural side of the business while Julie's award-winning skills are put to use for the firm's interior design needs. The team specializes in bespoke designs of all kinds—nothing is out of reach. Every home, every project, is completely unique and tailored to fit the site and the owner's vision. They focus on design axes, seamless indoor-outdoor living, natural beauty, and clean, easy living.

Sherí DeGeer Home - see pages 120-125

Sherí DeGeer
Beaverton, Oregon 97007
503.789.7867
Degeerinteriors.com

Sherí DeGeer began her interior design business in 2004 with a background in luxury goods and services. This, combined with being surrounded by the building industry her entire life, gave Sherí a strong foothold to launch her own firm. The eponymous company gives homeowners exactly what they want: an elegant space that is comfortable and reflects their tastes and lifestyles. Sherí places great emphasis on color and how it works in a room, so much so that she started her own paint line, Crown Jewel Luxury Paint, which launched in 2012. You'll find these rich, luxurious tones incorporated into all of her design projects.

SORA design - see pages 126-129

Katsuya Arai, Akiko Arai
Portland, OR 97229
971.408.6854
sora-design.info

At SORA design, the goal of each home is to improve the quality of life through architecture. Based in Portland, the husband-and wife-team is made up of Akiko and Katsuya Arai, and they see through all aspects of their projects together with a hands-on approach. Although the architects share a Japanese background, they don't design Japanese architecture per se, but their design solutions often incorporate traditional Japanese ideas: natural light, organic materials, and line of sight to enhance a space. Their spaces are simple and intentional, and come to life with the owner's individuality. Each home is highly customized to the homeowner.

WASHINGTON

Click Architects - see pages 132-137

Cheryl Click, Stephen Click
Seattle, WA
click-architects.com
instagram.com/click_architects/
206.291.6487

Click Architects specializes in modern, innovative residential design. Founded in 2013 by architects Cheryl and Stephen Click, they are guided by their passion for excellence and love for collaboration. Each unique project is molded by careful and deliberate consideration for site specifics, programmatic desire, and the unifying idea. Their collaborative process connects clients and project team members early on to help inform design decisions, guide budget and schedule, and maintain the underlying project goals. Staying true to their beliefs and working closely with their clients allows each project the opportunity to tell a different story.

CLT Design / Build - see pages 138-141

Craig Telgenhoff
179 Birch Bay Lynden Road, Suite A,
Lynden, WA 98264
360.961.6957
cltdesignbuild.com

Founded by chief architect Craig Telgenhoff, CLT Design/Build was established in 2002 to provide homeowners with unique design concepts and construction management services. The firm specializes in finely crafted residential and commercial projects. After years in the industry, Craig learned that there is no better builder than the person who designed the project. The design/build concept allows clients to have their on-site designer making informed design and construction decisions throughout the project. With a dedication to client service and the craft of architecture and construction, Craig and his team work with homeowners to find creative solutions to fit their site, personality, budget, and schedule.

David Pool Architecture - see pages 142-145

David Pool, AIA
Seattle/Tacoma, WA
253.651.4077
davidpoolarchitecture.com

David Pool Architecture is a renowned architectural firm specializing in modern luxury homes that capture the essence of the West Coast lifestyle. With a passion for creating unique and exceptional designs, David Pool strives to forge a deep emotional connection between his clients and their homes. His mission is to craft beautiful residences that reflect the individuality and aspirations of each family while harmoniously integrating with the natural surroundings of the project site. David is known for his commitment to delivering outstanding results through a thoughtful and creative design process. He firmly believe that a successful home design goes beyond aesthetics, encompassing functionality, sustainability, and a profound understanding of the homeowners' needs and desires.

Donnally Architects - see pages 130-131, 146-157

Bruce Donnally, AIA
135 1st Avenue West
Seattle, WA 98119
206.283.4699
donnallyarchitects.com

For Bruce Donnally, every design project starts with listening and learning. From there, he can discover creative, fresh ways to find the most elegant solutions that address the client's needs while also producing compelling buildings. His architectural approach is modern in the sense that it reflects current lifestyle choices, costs, and technologies. Nonetheless, when integrating new design elements into older buildings, he is committed to respecting the original historic style. A practicing architect for more than 40 years, Bruce received his bachelor's degree from the University of Virginia and his master's degree in architecture from Yale University.

First Lamp Architects - see pages 152-159

Taylor Callaway
4915 Rainier Avenue S, Suite 202
Columbia City, Seattle, WA 98118
206.240.0906
Firstlamp.net

Founder and lead architect Taylor Callaway first fell in love with architecture when he was just a boy, tagging along with a friend's dad to job sites. He still holds that same passion today and runs his firm with the core philosophy that meaningful buildings have a profound impact. Founded in 2009, First Lamp started with Taylor's idea that good architecture blends creativity with craftsmanship and fosters the connection between architecture, design, and construction. While First Lamp is a full-service architecture firm, it functioned as a design-build firm for the first 10 years. The team places emphasis on the end result: stunning, functional, net-zero homes that transcend ordinary design.

Island Architecture - see pages 160-163

Nina Pellar LeBaron, AIA
1905 Bay Place
Anacortes, WA 98221
360.378.7647
islandarchitecture.net

Nina Pellar LeBaron has been designing custom houses on the San Juan Islands since 2002. Before that, she was in the San Francisco Bay area, totaling 35 years of experience remodeling homes and creating new ones that look and feel as if they "belong." Her firm specializing in vernacular—a style that complements its surroundings—and green architecture to respect the site's natural beauty. Using 3-D models, Nina focuses on how a design works from the inside out, ensuring that the home's flow is effortless and highly functional right from the front door.

Kaplan Homes - see pages 160-163

Nathan Kaplan
Sedro-Woolley, WA 98284
360.540.7774
kaplanhomesunlimited.com

Kaplan Homes Unlimited is a residential and commercial construction company comprised of skilled, in-house artisans who have more than 100 years of collective experience. It offers a wide range of design-build services and promises open communication, customized service, and a timely response. A highly inclusive approach lets the KHU team explore new ideas and innovations, ensuring the best outcome for every project. At its core, KHU is a company that prioritizes collaboration and developing long-term relationships built on trust with clients, A/E partners, trade partners, and its communities.

MacPherson Construction & Design - see pages 164-173

Roger MacPherson
21626 SE 28th Street
Sammamish, WA 98075
425.391.3333
macphersonconstruction.com

Founded by Roger MacPherson in 1983, MacPherson Construction & Design is a creative, close-knit team based in Washington State. The passionate group of professionals takes pride in working together to reach a common goal and coordinate the countless details of each home. The firm specializes in custom design and construction, including interiors, which allows for a seamless transition between project phases. They get to know each of their clients on a personal level and work toward creating dream homes that reflect the families' lifestyles. MacPherson Construction & Design takes pride in each home and has built more than 180 waterfront homes in the Pacific Northwest.

BRITISH COLUMBIA

Cara Interiors - see pages 176-179

Cara Lawson, AKBD
12885 16 Avenue
Surrey, BC V4A 1N5, Canada
604.385.4011
carainteriors.com

Founder of Cara Interiors, principal designer Cara Lawson is in the business of making stunning first impressions. Cara holds her AKBD designation and is an accredited member of the National Kitchen & Bath Association. Her boutique firm embodies the idea that interior design should support the function, aesthetics, and culture of those that are living or working in the space. It is the perfect balance of psychology and the fine arts, equally functional, charming, and uplifting. Cara offers clients more than 20 years of experience and has been recognized as a Top 3 Interior Designer for Surrey B.C. and is a member of the Havan Canadian Home Builders Association.

DCYT Architecture - see pages 180-183

Dougles Cheung
3022 Cambie Street
Vancouver BC
778.233.9001
dcytarchitecture.ca/

Since its establishment in 1996 and under the leadership of the principal Douglas Cheung, DCYTA has slowly grown to a team of highly talented designers. With projects ranging from healthcare, commercial, and residential to interior design, DCYTA focuses its approach in maintaining a good balance between creativity and functionality. In addition, they believe great architecture comes from a thorough understanding and creative manipulation of construction materials and detailing. With these basic principles in mind, it has always been DCYTA's ultimate goal to design custom West Coast homes that bring clients' dreams to reality.

Hynesite Designs - see pages 184-187

Timea Hynes
West Vancouver, BC V7V0B6
604.265.6837
hynesitedesigns.com

Serving Vancouver and surrounding areas, Hynesite Designs is a boutique interior design firm run by owner and founder Timea Hynes. Her work aims to avoid fading trends and offers a timeless aesthetic that incorporates the homeowner's vision and lifestyle. Whether the project is big or small, Timea and her team strive to achieve something different and distinctly beautiful. The firm's services include 3-D renderings, full consultation, bathroom and custom vanity design, bedroom and closet design, kitchen design and custom cabinets, floorplans, home staging, living and dining room design, and much more. Each project is carefully navigated to result in a space that resonates with the client.

Intermind Design, Inc. - see pages 188-197

Mila Djuras
609 Lidster Place
New Westminster, BC, Canada V3L 5E2
604.338.9936
interminddesign.com

Mila Djuras, owner and founder of Vancouver-based Intermind Design, uses a comprehensive approach for every project and is known for coming up with creative solutions of the highest quality. As the principal of her heavily awarded firm, Mila and her close-knit team oversee every aspect of her projects, including architectural and interior design, management, and quality and budget control. Her uniquely merged, integrated design-build model lets each tradesperson and contractor who is working on the project understand the various angles at hand. The talented design team never shies away from challenges and resourcefully transforms them into opportunities to create lasting, innovative environments.

Isometrix Design, Inc. - see pages 198-201

Beatrice Hsu
#1918-1030 West Georgia Street
Vancouver, BC V6E 2Y3
604.729.0505
isometrixdesign.ca

Beatrice Hsu's work is as diverse as her cultural background. Founder and principal interior designer of Isometrix Design, Inc., Beatrice grew up in London, England with her German mother and Chinese father, who hailed from Hong Kong. She studied at London's Middlesex University and went on to work in London and Hong Kong doing luxury hospitality design before moving to Vancouver. She speaks several languages and infuses her international influences into the firm's projects. Interiors are about space, light, and beauty, in that order, and they should reflect who you are, she believes.

Step One Design - see pages 202-207

Michael Dunsmuir
Victoria, BC
778.433.1434
steponedesign.ca

With more than 25 years of experience in the residential design industry, Michael Dunsmuir has built a reputation for having creative, unique designs and highly detailed building plans. Step One Design is a Victoria-based firm that Michael runs with his wife and business partner, Lisa Dunsmuir. They utilize three-dimensional computer-aided models that reveal a home's design down to the smallest detail. It allows the Step One team and the homeowners to collaborate toward a shared, clear vision. Michael doesn't believe in simply checking all the boxes on the client's must-have list, but instead works methodically to create a highly customized home that reflects the homeowners' lifestyle.

Vineyard Development - see pages 208-211

Craig Mohr
1631 Dickson Avenue, Office #3, Suite 1800
Kelowna, BC, Canada, V1Y 0B5
250.878.9411
VineyardCustomHomes.ca

Vineyard Developments is a Kelowna-based firm that offers the unique start-to-finish service, or the full-circle advantage, as owner Craig Mohr calls it. Equipped with decades of experience, the team has the full-circle design knowledge and construction expertise to take projects from the first meeting to move-in day. Vineyard Developments serves as designer, project manager, builder, and sales person, so clients benefit by having a consistent point of contact and a common thread of understanding through each phase of the process. The firm operates on a simple, timeless policy by putting themselves in the clients' shoes. They're always prepared to fulfill the highest expectations.

www.ingramcontent.com/pod-product-compliance
Lightning Source LLC
Chambersburg PA
CBHW050738110526
44590CB00002B/18